THE PLOT WHISPERER *Workbook*

STEP-BY-STEP EXERCISES TO
Help You Create Compelling Stories

MARTHA ALDERSON, *Founder of PlotWriMo*

Avon, Massachusetts

Published by
Adams Media, a division of F+W Media, Inc.
57 Littlefield Street, Avon, MA 02322. U.S.A.
www.adamsmedia.com

ISBN 10: 1-4405-4274-0
ISBN 13: 978-1-4405-4274-9
eISBN 10: 1-4405-4384-4
eISBN 13: 978-1-4405-4384-5

Printed in the United States of America.

10   9   8   7   6

This publication is designed to provide accurate and authoritative information with regard to the subject matter covered. It is sold with the understanding that the publisher is not engaged in rendering legal, accounting, or other professional advice. If legal advice or other expert assistance is required, the services of a competent professional person should be sought.

—From a *Declaration of Principles* jointly adopted by a Committee of the American Bar Association and a Committee of Publishers and Associations

Many of the designations used by manufacturers and sellers to distinguish their product are claimed as trademarks. Where those designations appear in this book and Adams Media was aware of a trademark claim, the designations have been printed with initial capital letters.

This book is available at quantity discounts for bulk purchases.
For information, please call 1-800-289-0963.

Dedication

To the man who scanned the wall of his cherished library and always picked just the right book for me. That he believed the dyslexic little girl next to him could possibly read and enjoy his grown-up stories made me believe it myself.

My father, Samuel Welch Stockton.

CONTENTS

INTRODUCTION 7

PART I: *Preparation* 15

CHAPTER 1: **PREPARE TO PLOT** 17

CHAPTER 2: **CREATE COMPELLING CHARACTERS AND SPIRITED ACTION** 27

CHAPTER 3: **MAKING THE SCENE** 39

CHAPTER 4: **BUILD YOUR OWN PLOT PLANNER** 45

CHAPTER 5: **WHO'S YOUR PROTAGONIST?** 59

PART II: *Begin Plotting* 67

CHAPTER 6: **CREATE AN INTRODUCTION CHECKLIST** 69

CHAPTER 7: **BUILD THE OPENING SCENES** 81

CHAPTER 8: **BEGIN AT THE BEGINNING** 95

CHAPTER 9: **YOU'RE HALFWAY THERE** 107

CHAPTER 10: **THE CRISIS IS HERE** 131

CHAPTER 11: **WHAT ARE THE SUBPLOTS?** 149

CHAPTER 12: **WE'RE AT THE END** 157

PART III: *Analyzing Your Plot* 177

CHAPTER 13: **IT'S ABOUT CAUSE AND EFFECT** 179

CHAPTER 14: **FIND YOUR THEMATIC BUBBLE** 189

CHAPTER 15: **FINDING THE STRONGEST CLIMAX** 199

CHAPTER 16: **JUST WHO ARE YOUR CHARACTERS, ANYWAY?** 207

CHAPTER 17: **THE END OF THE BEGINNING AND THE BEGINNING OF THE END** 213

CONCLUSION 221

INTRODUCTION

You want to write a book. You stare at the screen in front of you, unsure how to proceed. Your tea tastes bitter. Your stomach seizes up.

It's not just that you need the words. You know, in general, what you want to say. You may even have some idea of how to say it. But what you *don't* have is a structure. You need a plot. Once you get it, you're confident you can fill in the words. But above all, you need a plot. This is what I can help you with.

The Plot Whisperer Workbook offers a series of hands-on, practical exercises for the plot and structure ideas found in *The Plot Whisperer: Secrets of Story Structure Any Writer Can Master*. The workbook focuses you tightly on the structural issues you'll need to address and the skills you'll need to master in order to develop a compelling plot. If you've not read *The Plot Whisperer*, I strongly recommend that before you go further you purchase a copy and go through it, since I'll refer back to many of the concepts I explored in that book.

The purpose of the workbook is to develop and expand the plot of your novel, memoir, or screenplay. In doing the following exercises, you'll establish a broad scope of the characters of your story and a deeper view of your plot, including three plot lines in particular:

- Character Emotional Development Plot
- Dramatic Action Plot
- Thematic Significance Plot

In *The Plot Whisperer*, I wanted to help you deal with what often feels like an emotional roller-coaster ride when you're plotting and writing a story from the beginning to end. I suggested that this personal journey for you often mirrors your protagonist's development. This companion workbook is devoted purely to the craft of plotting and devising a pleasing structure for your reader.

This workbook includes exercises I use in plot workshops I teach around the country. I developed these exercises after analyzing countless novels, memoirs, and screenplays. In these analyses, I used some basic tools I created for the workshops—in particular, the Plot Planner and the Scene Tracker. Over the years, I've created hundreds of Plot Planners and Scene Trackers for contemporary and classic bestsellers, blockbuster movie scripts, and moving memoirs.

You may be eager to write a novel, a memoir, or a screenplay and, at the same time, confused about where and how to begin. Perhaps you are stuck somewhere in the process of writing a story. Or you are a successfully published writer intent on producing a better book. This workbook clears a path for you in much the same way as I might do in a live workshop, where advanced writers work on their plots side by side with people who are coming to writing for the first time.

To all these people, I suggest that writing goes through three stages: imaginative, generative, and refinement.

1. In the imaginative phase of writing a story, when prompted to fill in a template or answer questions, search your imagination for hints of the plot elements discussed.
2. In the generative stage, integrate the plot elements discussed.
3. At the refinement stage, demand every plot element in every scene.

In other words: Imagine. Create. Test.

This applies to you no matter what stage of writing you're at. If you're just starting out, you'll devise a main character. For writers further along, you'll deepen your understanding and portrayal of the protagonist. You may identify antagonists, list scenes, and plot them on a Plot Planner. You'll need to imagine, create, and test the beginning and middle and end of your overall plot. Consider the themes and the thematic significance of your story. Explore the protagonist's backstory. Create a climax and then rewrite it again. Link scenes by cause and effect. Intensify spirited conflict, tension, and suspense.

In Part I of this workbook, we'll prepare all the elements necessary to create the plot of your story. In Part II, you begin plotting the beginning, middle, and end. Part III is devoted to analyzing what you developed in the first two parts. In each chapter, I'll explain how the process works. Then I'll give you an example of plot planning based on a work of literature. Finally, I'll invite you to apply these lessons to a blank Plot Planner and Scene Tracker.

As you work your way through the exercises in this workbook, you'll watch your story emerge. At the end of the process, you'll hold the backbone of your story development. Refer to the workbook as you write your story. Use it before you make any major revision. Revisit and remember the steps you took to get from inspiration to a finished story.

The tools I've given you here are the best ones I know of to demonstrate just what's going on in a plot. A Plot Planner is a visual line that represents the invisible energy of the Universal Story, showing the stages through which the characters move in order to complete their story. Whereas the Plot Planner supports you in analyzing your plot at the overall story level, the Scene Tracker allows you to analyze your plot at the scene level. Both templates are visual aids to help you plot your story in a way that pleases you and ultimately satisfies your readers, too.

There is no right or wrong when using these tools. Remember: You can always erase what you've written in the workbook and start again. (I'd recommend using a pencil rather than a pen when you're going through the workbook for precisely that reason.) It often takes a couple of attempts to string your story's elements along the Plot Planner's basic line before you're confident you've got the right ideas and the right organization. The first couple of times you do it, you may find that you need to move scenes to another place in the story. That's fine. That's what's supposed to happen. Every time you fill in a Plot Planner, you see your story from a different angle and push in directions you never thought of before.

Don't be afraid to step back and get some perspective on what you're writing. See how all the scenes work together against the backdrop of the entire piece. This is where the Scene Tracker as well as the Plot Planner can give you a unique look into the causality between scenes and the overall coherence and deeper meaning of your story. At some point in the process, you'll find your Eureka moment. With your story spread out on a Plot Planner in front of you, the significance of your characters and the dramatic action of your story will shine through. Yes, you'll say to yourself, there really *is* a point to this story. Yes, the characters really *would* do that. With such an insight, you can turn scenes with emotionally rich characters experiencing conflict into the driving force behind an exceptional story.

The exercises in this workbook are not going to write your story, but they will give your writing a solid direction; which, in turn, stimulates more consistent writing. At any point you feel inspired to write, stop working on the exercises and write. Return to them when you become stumped or discouraged or curious about what comes next in the development of the plot and structure of your story. Rather than let your story crumble, give it the foundation it needs.

If, at any point in the process of completing the exercises in this workbook, your energy for your work flags, I suggest you refer to *The Plot Whisperer* to discover why some of the concepts may come easily for you while other ideas tend to feel overwhelming.

For our work here, bring your ideas. When you gain a firm understanding of the natural trajectory of a story and why certain scenes in specific spots are critical and necessary, you'll find that this knowledge stimulates more ideas. They migrate from your imagination to the page. Instead of languishing with a half-finished story, the exercises in this workbook push you to the end. Once you've completed your story (but before you offer your work for others to read), use the space provided in the workbook to test your plot and structure.

It takes time and a deep intellectual and emotional commitment to write a book. Plot and structure allow your characters the freedom to do what they want. Rather than manipulate your characters, forcing them into the needs of your plot, if you stick to a time-honored structure, you will find your characters working with you and revealing truths you may not have imagined by yourself. Your characters willingly take part in the process.

Figure 1. The Plot Planner: Above and Below

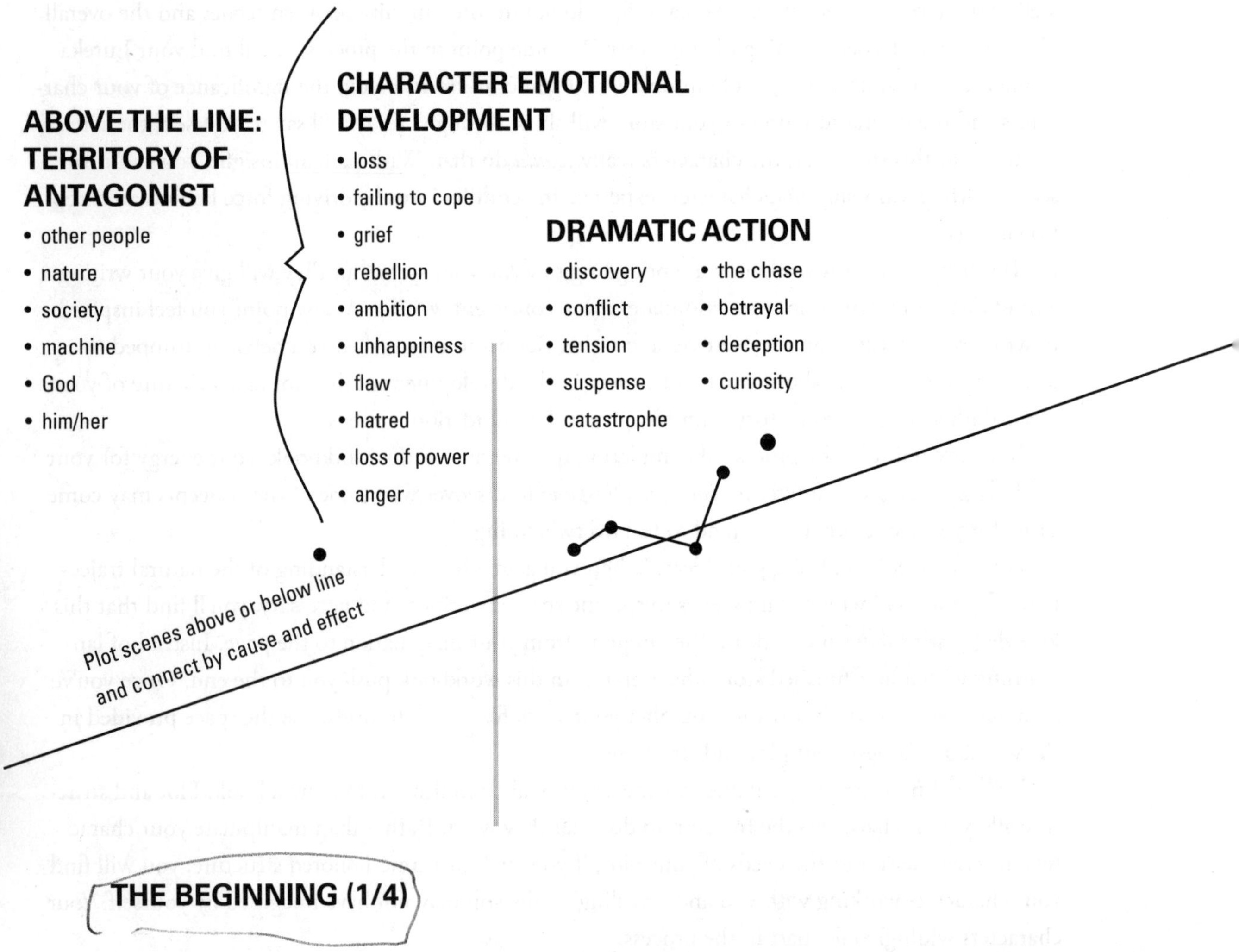

CHARACTER EMOTIONAL DEVELOPMENT

ABOVE THE LINE: TERRITORY OF ANTAGONIST

- other people
- nature
- society
- machine
- God
- him/her

- loss
- failing to cope
- grief
- rebellion
- ambition
- unhappiness
- flaw
- hatred
- loss of power
- anger

DRAMATIC ACTION

- discovery
- conflict
- tension
- suspense
- catastrophe

- the chase
- betrayal
- deception
- curiosity

Plot scenes above or below line
and connect by cause and effect

THE BEGINNING (1/4)

THEMATIC SIGNIFICANCE

- mood
- metaphor
- sensory details
- setting
- define
- development
- mention

DRAMATIC ACTION

- lull in conflict
- giving info
- telling

CHARACTER EMOTIONAL DEVELOPMENT

- calm
- coping
- planning
- solving problems
- contemplative
- in control

BELOW THE LINE: TERRITORY OF PROTAGONIST

THE MIDDLE (1/2)

THE END (1/4)

Figure 2. Scene Tracker Template
Copyright © 2004, Martha Alderson

Project Name:

Date:

Draft:

SCENE TRACKER

Chapter:

Scene/ Summary	Dates/Setting	Character Emotional Development	Goal
SCENE 1			
SCENE 2			
SCENE 3			
OPTIONAL			
OPTIONAL			

Notes:

Dramatic/ Action Plot	Conflict	Emotional Change	Thematic Significance/Details

PART I

Preparation

CHAPTER 1

PREPARE TO PLOT

Plot Whisperer Tweet: *First couple of drafts? For now, forget the particulars. Concentrate instead on the broad principles of plot and structure.*

What is plot? Plot is how the events in a story directly impact the main character.

People are often surprised to find that character development is a central part of plot. In all great books the protagonist's emotional development and the story's dramatic action become so interwoven that it is often difficult to separate them.

Three intertwining primary plot lines are in every good story:

1. Character Emotional Development/Transformation (CED)
2. Dramatic Action (DA)
3. Thematic Significance (TS)

Fundamentally, every plot has the following structure: A character pursues a goal. She faces a series of conflicts and obstacles, and as a result her choices change over time. In the end, she is transformed, and her ultimate transformation creates her anew with a different understanding of herself and her existence.

Always, in the best-written stories, characters are emotionally affected by events. In great stories, the dramatic action transforms characters. It's this transformation that makes a story meaningful.

Figure 3. Character Emotional Development Transformation for Aibileen
The Help , a novel by Kathryn Stockett and screenplay by Tate Taylor

Transformation Summary

At the beginning of the novel and screenplay, Aibileen (A) is a timid maid, unwilling and unable to fight against the unreasonable and unfair treatment she receives from her employer as she serves the status quo. By the end of the story, she has transformed into a courageous woman who shrugs off the socially acceptable role of maid to embrace independence and true freedom.

Character Emotional Development

(CED) A acts in the expected role of the subservient, obedient maid.

She expects to be treated poorly by her employer and to work hard for very little money.

She is proud of her skills in raising other women's children and keeping a tidy house.

Dramatic Action

(DA) A helps S write housekeeping column. She refuses to help S with her book.

Character Significance

(TS) Societal rules define acceptable behavior versus what actions, when taken outside the norm, are subject to punishment.

(CED) A's desire to tell her story is greater than her fear of being caught. The book project empowers her.

She gives her opinion when asked by her employer, something she would never have done previously.

(DA) S and A work on the book at A's house.

(TS) The same societal rules that define acceptable behavior also define the appropriate punishment when someone steps out of line.

THE BEGINNING (1/4)

(CED) A's fear grows.

We learn more about her son.

A blames white men for his death.

(DA) Angered by the unfair sentencing of a fellow maid and friend, all the maids arrive at A's house to tell their stories to S.

A's employer threatens to fire her if she speaks to S again.

(TS) The lines between acceptable behavior and unacceptable behavior grow to include those lines between husbands and wives, white and black, employers and the help.

(CED) A tells S the truth about Constantine.

A teaches her young ward to love all people with no regard to their skin color.

(DA) With the little money A earns from the book, she quits her job as a maid to write the housekeeping column at the newspaper—two things she could never have done at the beginning of the book.

(TS) By breaking society's rules, A's dream of being a writer comes true.

She gains true freedom.

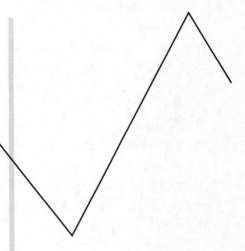

KEY:
(CED): Character Emotional Development
(DA): Dramatic Action
(TS): Thematic Significance

THE MIDDLE (1/2)   **THE END (1/4)**

Figure 4. Character Emotional Development Transformation for Eugenia "Skeeter" Phelan, *The Help*, a novel by Kathryn Stockett and screenplay by Tate Taylor

Transformation Summary

At the beginning of the story, Eugenia "Skeeter" Phelan (S) acts as the woman she was raised and is expected to be by her past. By the end of the book, she transforms into an independent and courageous woman who chooses her own path, one outside the norm, to her future.

(CED) S returns home from college in 1962 to act as expected of a proper Southern lady: She plays bridge with the other young women in town; dates men, hoping to satisfy Mother's expectation to marry, and writes a housekeeping advice column, though she knows nothing about keeping house.

She keeps secret her dream of becoming a writer.

(DA)A NY editor is willing to read S's book made up of maid narratives.

(TS) Societal rules define acceptable behavior versus what actions, when taken outside the norm, may be subject to punishment.

(CED) S continues to agree to things she would rather not do, such as go on a blind date, succumb to her mother's wishes that she tame her unruly curls, and attend Junior League.

(DA) S and A work on the book at A's house.

S lies to one of her powerful friends.

(TS) S is pressured to conform to society when her friends begin snubbing her in public.

THE BEGINNING (1/4)

(CED) S finds out why her maid unexpectedly left. By writing the book and choosing a different path than the one she was brought up to follow, S learns how courageous and independent she is truly becoming.

(DA) Book must be finished at year's end and include a section about S's maid. S's fiancé withdraws proposal upon learning truth about the book. S's mother compliments S for being just who she is.

(TS) S's childhood friends represent the old world order. S represents transformation and change in the new world.

(CED) S stands up to powerful friend.

(DA) Well aware of severe punishment for her involvement with the maids, S works harder to complete book.

(TS) S is ostracized for her beliefs; thrown out of League and bridge club. Everyone agrees never again to speak to her.

KEY:
(CED): Character Emotional Development
(DA): Dramatic Action
(TS): Thematic Significance

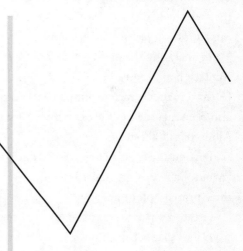

THE MIDDLE (1/2)　　　　　　　　**THE END (1/4)**

When you get stuck while writing a story, it is usually because you're ignoring one or more of the three plot elements I mentioned. You're doing this by:

- Concentrating on action only, forgetting that character provides interest and is the primary reason that people go to the movies and read books
- Organizing everything solely around the character and overlooking the fact that dramatic action provides the excitement every story needs
- Neglecting to develop the overall meaning and thematic significance of the story

To ensure you do not fall prey to any of these writer pitfalls, let's examine together how a protagonist (the character most changed by the dramatic action) is transformed over time using the three major plot lines. We'll start with *The Help,* Kathryn Stockett's wildly successful debut novel that was later adapted as a screenplay by Tate Taylor and made into an award-winning film starring Emma Stone, Octavia Spencer, and Viola Davis. *The Help* is about the unlikely friendship that develops between two women separated by societal rules who nonetheless partner to write a book. In doing so, they tell the world the truth about the lives of black maids working in white Southern homes in the early 1960s in Jackson, Mississippi.

In analyzing the plot lines of *The Help,* I have included both of the two main characters, Aibileen and Skeeter, because each of them is transformed by the dramatic action in the story. (A third main character, Minnie, goes through an equally dramatic transformation and could have also been included in the exercise, but for the sake of clarity and space, I focus the exercise only on Aibileen and Skeeter.)

Beyond the character emotional development transformation summary for both characters, I also lay out, on a separate transformation cycle Plot Planner—one for each character—a summary of the three primary plot lines.

Create a separate transformation cycle plot planner for each main character.

A Plot Planner is simply a visual representation of how the three plot lines rise and fall in a story, following the path of the Universal Story. The Universal Story is the rhythm of life and reflects the spark in all things to awaken to consciousness. To understand the rhythm of life and the Universal Story is to see them as the same energetic path toward dying off, moving forward, dying off, and moving forward over and over again.

At the end of the chapter, you'll discover and explain the transformation the protagonist in your story undergoes as well as the three major plot lines your story embodies. If you do not yet have a firm story idea in mind, complete the exercise using a story example(s) of your own choice.

This exercise is worth doing several times, both on your story and on someone else's book. Choose a favorite of yours, a book you reread, and learn why you love it. Do another author's work a couple of times and then do your own. As you do it, you'll discover that the three plot lines will, almost magically, rise out of the words on the page and reveal themselves to you. The more you do this kind of analysis, the more it will become second nature to you, and the stronger your own plots will become.

Your Turn

Now it's your chance to do the kind of analysis you saw in Figures 3 and 4 regarding *The Help*. Remember: You can try this out first on a favorite book or story before turning to your own work. In this Plot Planner, you're going to:

1. Summarize the Character Emotional Development/Transformation Cycle for the protagonist of your story. (If you have more than one main character, complete the exercise for each one—just as I did for both Aibileen and Skeeter.)
2. Plot out how the character and the action and the themes grow and change over time through the three major plot lines.

CHARACTER EMOTIONAL DEVELOPMENT/TRANSFORMATION CYCLE

Discover the transformational cycle the protagonist in your story undergoes throughout the three major plot lines. If you do not yet have a firm story idea in mind, complete the exercise using a story example(s) of your choice, preferably one that has won awards or received some other form of critical acclaim.

Fill in each of the three major plot lines at each of the major parts of the story. For now, think in broad terms about how the character and the action and the themes grow and change over time. Jot your ideas in the space provided.

Figure 5. Character Emotional Development Transformation

Transformation Summary

_____

_____

_____

_____

_____

KEY:

(CED): Character Emotional Development

(DA): Dramatic Action

(TS): Thematic Significance

(CED) _____

_____

(CED) _____

_____

(DA) _____

_____

(DA) _____

_____

(TS) _____

_____

(TS) _____

_____

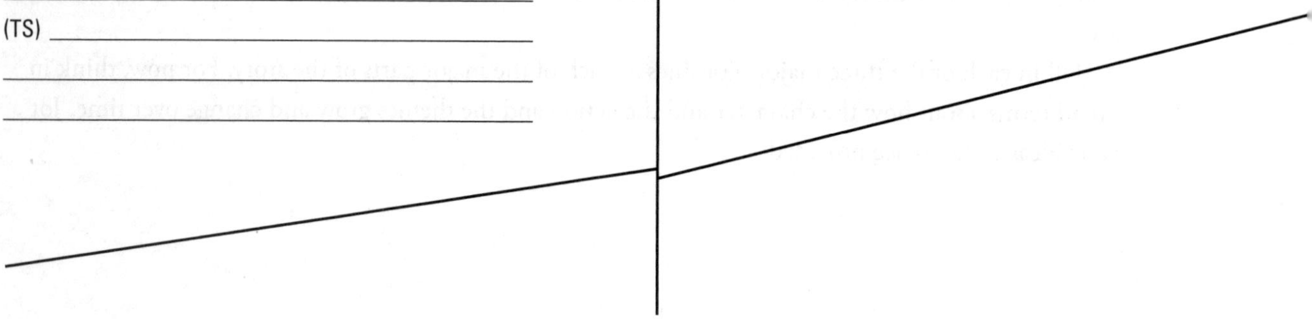

THE BEGINNING (1/4)

(CED) _____
_____
_____
_____
_____
(DA) _____
_____
_____
_____
(TS) _____
_____
_____
_____

(CED) _____
_____
(DA) _____
_____
(TS) _____
_____
_____

THE MIDDLE (1/2)   **THE END (1/4)**

CHAPTER 2

CREATE COMPELLING CHARACTERS AND SPIRITED ACTION

Plot Whisperer Tweet: *Character Emotional Development is cumulative, based on all the scenes over time, and is long-term & transformative.*

Behind each character is a world only she sees and imagines. The trick to creating a memorable character is finding that something special in or about her that makes her "her." Challenge yourself to shape your character to reflect unique feelings, ones perhaps that show life differently than those traditionally depicted in stories. Only she feels about her life the way she does. Only she sees and hears the world around her in the way she does. Such individuality creates a sense of mystery around each character.

As we saw in the introduction, two major templates in this workbook are the Plot Planner and Scene Tracker. These two templates display scenes from novel, memoir, and screenplay examples to show how plot and structure works. You are invited to fill in Plot Planner and Scene Tracker templates to discover and explore the plot and structure using scenes from your own story. First, however, before you can create scenes to plot out on the templates, you must gather personal information only the characters can reveal.

Begin by developing the character's front story information only for now. The front story is the story that drives the action in the scene on the page. Later in the workbook, you are prompted to explore your character's backstory information both in Chapter 5, "Who's Your Protagonist?" and her backstory wound in Chapter 16, "Just Who Are Your Characters, Anyway?"

For now, let's concentrate on getting the front story going. The plot of a story is about a character faced with a series of conflicts and obstacles while in pursuit of a goal, which, over time, inspire her to change her choices. In the end, she is transformed, and her ultimate transformation creates her anew with a different understanding of herself and her existence.

For you to write about a character pursuing her goal, you first need to know what her goals are. Before you know how her choices will change, you must discover what motivates her choices to begin with. To write about a character's transformation, you first must appreciate how she views herself and the world around her now, at the beginning of the story.

The thread that keeps the reader hooked is the tension in not knowing what the protagonist will do (her choices) when confronted with the next impossible scenario. The reader thinks she knows and reads on to learn if she is right or if the story will shift into a new, though foreshadowed, direction.

We want to "see" how she reacts, of course, not be told. Scenes with conflict, tension, suspense, or curiosity where the protagonist is not in control are where the energy surges and the story comes alive. These pieces make up a thematically linked whole and lead to a thematically significant ending.

Character Emotional Development/Transformation Profile

A Character Emotional Development/Transformation (CED) profile assists you in identifying who your character(s) is and what she wants at the beginning of the story, at the middle of the story, and at the end of the story.

Her goals reflect what she feels called to do. For some characters, her goals are hidden even to herself. For others, her goals come early and practically unfold of their own accords. Some character goals are singular and exclusive to her perceived needs. For other characters, her goals can change and follow new directions as she follows new directions, especially when she leaves the beginning of the story and enters the middle.

Often stories revolve around more than one main character who goes through a major change or transformation due to the dramatic action in the story (as in our example for *The Help* in Chapter 1). Each major character's goals and traits influence the primary plot as reflected on their own individual CED profile.

Often stories have a major antagonist who can act as an actual villain. This character, too, has goals and traits that influence the primary plot lines as reflected on her own individual CED profile.

Character Emotional Development/Transformation Profile

Major Pettigrew's Last Stand by Helen Simonson
Protagonist's name: Major Ernest Pettigrew, Englishman and widower

Dramatic Action Plot:

1. What is this character's goal?
   - **Upon entering the beginning of the story:** To reunite the two-gun set split by his father between his two sons, one of whom is recently deceased (this goal remains consistent throughout the entire story)
   - **Upon entering the middle of the story:** Escort Mrs. Ali to the annual club dance
   - **Upon entering the end of the story:** To win back Mrs. Ali
2. What stands in the way of the character achieving his goal?
   - **Upon entering the beginning of the story:** His grief over his younger brother's recent death and the resistance he meets with his sister-in-law Marjorie
   - **Upon entering the middle of the story:** His neighbors and friends
   - **Upon entering the end of the story:** Mrs. Ali's family and her beliefs about family
3. What does the character stand to lose if he does not achieve his goal?
   - **Upon entering the beginning of the story:** His belief that others will appreciate tradition and take what he believes is right action
   - **Upon entering the middle of the story:** His neighbors and friends and way of life
   - **Upon entering the end of the story:** The love of his life

Character Emotional Development Plot:

1. **What is the character's flaw or greatest fault?** Having never challenged the status quo and his naiveté about his friends and neighbors and community, set in his ways

2. **What is the character's greatest strength?** Loyalty (this strength ends up turning on him when his old friends turn against him), unwaveringly proper

3. **What does the character hate?** Change, most things modern

4. **What does the character love?** Literature, honor, tradition, duty, decorum, and a properly brewed cup of tea

5. **What is the character's greatest fear?** Change

6. **What is the character's dream?** To own both hunting guns and have even Lord Dagenham himself admire the pair

7. **What is the character's secret?** He is secretly pleased at the thought of reuniting the guns upon his brother's death.

CHARACTER PROFILE FOR MAJOR SECONDARY CHARACTERS

Character Emotional Development/Transformation Profile
Character's name: Mrs. Jasmina Ali, born in England; she is the Pakistani shopkeeper from the village and a widow

Dramatic Action Plot
1. What is this character's goal?
   - **Upon entering the beginning of the story:** To determine if going against family opinion is worth the struggle if the result of breaking with tradition is the loss of family—meaning should she give up her shop to her husband's family? Her late husband, in an act that defied tradition, left the shop to her.
   - **Upon entering the middle of the story:** To discuss Kipling with Major Pettigrew
   - **Upon entering the end of the story:** To forget Major Pettigrew
2. What stands in the way of the character achieving her goal?
   - **Upon entering the beginning of the story:** The influence of her father and his love of books, her husband's wish for her to keep the shop, her husband's family demanding she give up the store.
   - **Upon entering the middle of the story:** Her grandnephew George interferes with her ongoing struggle about what to do with the shop. Her nephew Abdul Wahid stands in her way of spending time with the major.
   - **Upon entering the end of the story:** Her love for the major

3. What does the character stand to lose if she does not achieve her goal?
   - **Upon entering the beginning of the story:** All her hopes and dreams
   - **Upon entering the middle of the story:** Love and companionship in her life
   - **Upon entering the end of the story:** Joy and happiness

Character Emotional Development Plot:

1. **What is the character's flaw or greatest fault?** Giving in to family pressure
2. **What is the character's greatest strength?** Blending tea, crisp enunciation, languages, honesty, driving like a man
3. **What does the character hate?** Being viewed as an invisible foreigner, status quo
4. **What does the character love?** Literature, reading, refusal to bow before authority, the world of books, George, Major Pettigrew
5. **What is the character's greatest fear?** Losing the shop and becoming an invisible babysitter
6. **What is the character's dream?** To live in a real Sussex cottage
7. **What is the character's secret?** Her father had a library of books that were burned by family.

CHARACTER PROFILE FOR THE MAJOR ANTAGONIST

Character Emotional Development/Transformation Profile
Character's name: Village society

Dramatic Action Plot
1. What is this character's goal?
   - **Upon entering the beginning of the story:** To retain the status quo of the community
   - **Upon entering the middle of the story:** To retain the status quo of the community
   - **Upon entering the end of the story:** To retain the status quo of the community
2. What stands in the way of the character achieving his/her goal?
   - **Upon entering the beginning of the story:** Change, progress
   - **Upon entering the middle of the story:** Change, progress
   - **Upon entering the end of the story:** Change, progress

3. What does the character stand to lose if he/she does not achieve his/her goal?
   - **Upon entering the beginning of the story:** The traditional way of life
   - **Upon entering the middle of the story:** The traditional way of life
   - **Upon entering the end of the story:** The traditional way of life

Character Emotional Development Plot

1. **What is the character's flaw or greatest fault?** Narrow-minded, exclusive, and the belief that that exclusiveness is " . . . a social thing and nothing to do with color"
2. **What is the character's greatest strength?** Ladies who "proudly speak of '. . . our dear Paki-stani friends at the shop' as proof that Edgecombe St. Mary was a utopia of multicultural understanding"
3. **What does the character hate?** Change
4. **What does the character love?** " . . . trinity of ladies going about the business of controlling all social and civic life in the village" and following "accepted rituals"
5. **What is the character's greatest fear?** Full integration, "what the world was coming to . . . "
6. **What is the character's dream?** To be like Mrs. Ali's belief that the power of the greatest views in the world comes not from being vast or exotic but ". . . from the knowledge that they do not change. You look at them and you know they have been the same for a thousand years."
7. **What is the character's secret?** Change is the death of the status quo.

Your Turn

If you are just starting to write a story or are weary of the one you've been laboring over, fill out the following forms based on a favorite story of yours, preferably one you find yourself returning to read again and again. Solidify your ideas by completing a separate CED profile for each major character(s) who goes through a change or transformation due to the dramatic action in your story:

Character Emotional Development/Transformational Profile

THE PROTAGONIST
Major viewpoint characters:

Antagonist(s)

Protagonist's name: _____

Dramatic Action Plot: _____

_____

Dramatic Action Plot
1. What is this character's goal?
- Upon entering the beginning of the story:

_____

- Upon entering the middle of the story:

_____

- Upon entering the end of the story:

_____

2. What stands in the way of the character achieving his/her goal?
- Upon entering the beginning of the story:

_____

- Upon entering the middle of the story:

_____

- Upon entering the end of the story:

_____

3. What does the character stand to lose if he/she does not achieve his/her goal?
- Upon entering the beginning of the story:

_____

- Upon entering the middle of the story:

_____

- Upon entering the end of the story:

_____

Character Emotional Development/Plot

1. What is the character's flaw or greatest fault?

_____
_____
_____

2. What is the character's greatest strength?

_____
_____
_____

3. What does the character hate?

_____
_____
_____

4. What does the character love?

_____
_____
_____

5. What is the character's greatest fear?

_____
_____
_____

6. What is the character's dream?

_____
_____
_____

7. What is the character's secret?

_____
_____
_____

Character Emotional Development/Transformational Profile

SECONDARY CHARACTERS

Character's name: _____

Dramatic action plot: _____

_____

_____

Dramatic Action Plot

1. What is this character's goal?
 - Upon entering the beginning of the story:

_____

 - Upon entering the middle of the story:

_____

 - Upon entering the end of the story:

_____

2. What stands in the way of the character achieving his/her goal?
 - Upon entering the beginning of the story:

_____

 - Upon entering the middle of the story:

_____

 - Upon entering the end of the story:

_____

3. What does the character stand to lose if he/she does not achieve his/her goal?
 - Upon entering the beginning of the story:

_____

 - Upon entering the middle of the story:

_____

 - Upon entering the end of the story:

_____

Character Emotional Development/Plot

1. What is the character's flaw or greatest fault?

_____

_____

_____

2. What is the character's greatest strength?

_____

_____

_____

3. What does the character hate?

_____

_____

_____

4. What does the character love?

_____

_____

_____

5. What is the character's greatest fear?

_____

_____

_____

6. What is the character's dream?

_____

_____

_____

7. What is the character's secret?

_____

_____

_____

Character Emotional Development/Transformational Profile

MAJOR ANTAGONIST
Character's name: _____

Dramatic action plot
1. What is this character's goal?
 - Upon entering the beginning of the story:

 _____
 - Upon entering the middle of the story:

 _____
 - Upon entering the end of the story:

 _____

2. What stands in the way of the character achieving his/her goal?
 - Upon entering the beginning of the story:

 _____
 - Upon entering the middle of the story:

 _____
 - Upon entering the end of the story:

 _____

3. What does the character stand to lose if he/she does not achieve his/her goal?
 - Upon entering the beginning of the story:

 _____
 - Upon entering the middle of the story:

 _____
 - Upon entering the end of the story:

 _____

Character Emotional Development/Plot

1. What is the character's flaw or greatest fault?

_____

_____

_____

2. What is the character's greatest strength?

_____

_____

_____

3. What does the character hate?

_____

_____

_____

4. What does the character love?

_____

_____

_____

5. What is the character's greatest fear?

_____

_____

_____

6. What is the character's dream?

_____

_____

_____

7. What is the character's secret?

_____

_____

_____

CHAPTER 3
MAKING THE SCENE

Plot Whisperer Tweet: *Strive always for meaning in what you write.*

In a scene a character acts and reacts to people, places, and events. In this respect, scenes are the basic building blocks of your story. But, as with any structure, if you have the wrong scenes or if they're assembled incorrectly, your story can—unexpectedly—collapse.

In this chapter you'll generate and analyze scenes for your story. If you have a draft of your story, use the scenes you've written. If you haven't finished a draft, use what you have and generate the rest. As with the other exercises in this book, it may be helpful for you to try the exercise using scenes from a beloved book or story.

If you have no scene ideas, consider what your character wants and then visualize the steps the character will take to get what she wants. As you imagine your story, use the goals that you listed in Chapter 2. Imagine scenes that show her thwarted at every turn.

For now, do not concern yourself with the specific elements in each scene. Simply generate scenes that show your main character moving forward for a specific purpose and the challenges she faces along the way.

As you visualize scenes for your story, slow down the story pace. Take your time exploring ideas. A scene stretches time with details; it reveals. Above all, scene shows rather than tells. Action and dialogue are scene markers. For now, do not worry about the content of the scenes. Simply consider the major events that happen in the story. Break those event ideas into scenes.

Events Create Scenes

A major turning point in the plot line of *The Help* occurs when Yule May is arrested for stealing a ring. Many scenes are required for the buildup to this turning point. Following the main event, other scenes show the effect the arrest has on the other plot lines. One scene in particular highlights the primary plot line: Skeeter's and Aibileen's goal of writing the book.

We see Skeeter "walk[ing] up Aibileen's steps at eight o'clock that night. This was supposed to be our first interview with Yule May and even though I know that's not going to happen, I've decided to come anyway.

"The room goes unbearably quiet again. The air is hot and smells like burned coffee. I feel a profound singularity here, in a place where I've almost grown comfortable. I feel the heat of dislike and guilt." One of the maids steps forward and volunteers to help Skeeter with her book. Then another maid volunteers. One by one, ten other maids tell her they want to help, too.

"The room clears out, except for Minny. She stands in the far corner, arms clamped across her chest. When everyone is gone, she looks up and meets my gaze for hardly a second then jerks her eyes to the brown curtains, pinned tight across the window. But I see it, the flicker on her mouth, a hint of softness beneath her anger. Minny has made this happen."

In this short scene, the tide of the story turns. Skeeter and Aibileen move nearer to the successful completion of their goal while also moving nearer (though they don't yet know it) to disaster. The construction of this paramount scene in the primary plot outlines for the reader all the horrid details lining up against Yule May now that she is in police custody and mirrors all the punishments waiting to befall any or all the maids—Skeeter, too—for involving themselves in the book.

The scene shows everyone in the room feeling the risks.

"The room is dead quiet. Everyone knows it: I glance around at the people in the room, their heads bowed as if looking at me might burn them. I look down. Nonetheless, everyone commits."

Scene Length

A scene can span a sentence or last an entire book. However, for the most part scenes should be relatively short, making them easy for readers to digest. For scenes that go on for pages, break them into smaller vignettes for ease in tracking them on a Scene Tracker and plotting them on a Plot Planner.

In *Major Pettigrew's Last Stand*, the scenes leading up to, during, and directly following the Golf Club dance cover pages and pages of the book. My own feeling is that the crisis plays out for too many pages. Actual moments in the story from the major picking up Mrs. Ali for the dance to their arrival at the country club to dinner served, followed by dancing which leads to an interpretive dance performance and a skit unfold in several scenes that are tightly linked by cause and effect. During these several scenes that lead up to the crisis of the story, we feel tension building in the clubhouse. The antagonists surrounding the major and Mrs. Ali at the party do not cause the true division between the major and Mrs. Ali. Ultimately, the major's insensitivity and denial are what split them apart. His ego gets in his way of spotting the trouble, as does his refusal to consciously acknowledge the closed minds of the status quo in and around him.

As much destruction as the action in these scenes does to the romance plot and the major's personal plot to accept change, it does a clever job of showing—not telling—the origins of the pair of fine English sporting guns the major has spent most of his life thinking about and attempting to reunite. These guns form the thematic basis of his backstory wound: His father broke with tradition and separated the guns, rather than performing the age-old traditional rite of handing down the set to the major. Reclaiming the guns into his full possession as the firstborn son is the goal that motivates much of the major's behavior throughout the front story. Such a thematically rich object as this pair of hunting guns holds sufficient energy that each time the object reappears or is mentioned the story builds in meaning and excitement.

The chaos of these scenes stands in direct contrast to the calm and gentle relationship the major and Mrs. Ali have been developing. The further chaos in the scene that follows mirrors the growing tension between the major and Mrs. Ali and foreshadows their coming split.

A long scene such as those described previously becomes cumbersome to analyze. Instead, use your own discretion and break the scene into more manageable parts.

List of Scenes

In the following exercise you will:

1. Identify scenes.
2. Create titles that best encapsulate the scenes.

The object here is to identify scenes that advance the story.

Because this workbook is about plotting your story, resist the temptation to write the story in this workbook. Instead, for your work here, summarize the essence of the scenes.

Write your scenes in manuscript form elsewhere. For your work here, create scene titles instead. Here's an example of what I mean.

SCENES FROM *ESPERANZA RISING*

Following is a list of scenes from the beginning of the award-winning middle grade novel *Esperanza Rising* by Pam Munoz Ryan. The novel is set during the time of the American Great Depression and is about a young Mexican girl, whose sense of self is stripped when she and her mother are forced to leave their life of privilege in Mexico for an uncertain future in the United States as farm workers.

SCENE LIST

The Beginning

Chapter 1: 1924

Scene 1: Father and Esperanza (E) feel the earth breathe.

Chapter 2: Las Uvas (Grapes)

Scene 2: E cuts the first grape cluster for the annual harvest at El Rancho de las Rosas.

Scene 3: E. awaits Father's arrival in the garden and pricks her finger (foreshadowing).

Scene 4: Abuelita teaches E. though the art of crocheting not to be afraid to start over (foreshadowing).

Scene 5: E's father's dead body is brought home.

Chapter 3: Las Papayas (Papayas)

Scene 6: The reality of her father's death sinks in.

Scene 7: E. opens the last birthday present from her father—a porcelain doll. (This doll becomes the thematically rich object and symbolizes both Esperanza's backstory wound and all she must surrender.)

Scene 8: E's mother, Mama, rejects Tio Luis's proposal of marriage.

Scene 9: E. and her childhood friend "stand on different sides of the river."

Scene 10: E. struggles to grasp the truth of the changes coming to her young life.

Chapter 4: Los Higos (Pigs)
Scene 11: El Rancho de las Rosas burns.
Scene 12: E. understands the future she imagined for herself is over.
Scene 13: Mama agrees to consider Tio Luis's proposal of marriage.
Scene 14: Mama commits to leave for California to work in the fields.
Scene 15: Mama and E. say goodbye to Abuelita. E. faces the reality of her poverty.
Scene 16: Mama accepts Tio Luis's proposal of marriage to procure a wagon for their use.

The End of the Beginning
Scene 17: In the cover of night, Mama and E. leave their home for good.

Chapter 5: La Guayabas (Guavas)
Scene 18: They begin their escape to California hidden in a secret compartment of the wagon.
Scene 19: On the train on the next leg of their journey, E. refuses to surrender her elevated view of herself as better than those around her and is punished by Mama's disapproval of her.

Your Turn

In analyzing *Esperanza Rising,* we created a list of the novel's scenes (we only went a couple of scenes past the one-quarter mark and into the middle of the story). For your exercise, I want you to list your scenes all the way to the end of your story. Shorten scene titles while still capturing the major plot elements of the scene. Each scene title should take up no more than one line of the following scene list.

It's not necessary for you to have written all (or any) of your scenes. Just list scene ideas in the order in which you envision them landing in your story. If your book is made up of many small chapters, each one encapsulating a scene, list events in the story by chapter.

The trick to this exercise is *not* to see how many scenes you can list. Instead, you want to identify and list scenes that advance the story on a multitude of plot levels.

Remember that it may take you several tries before you get the list in an order that satisfies you. For this reason, I recommend using a pencil instead of a pen, so you can erase parts of your first ordering and move scenes around. Also remember that it's often a good idea to try out this exercise using scenes from a favorite book. The more you practice this analysis and construction, the better you'll get at it.

List of Scenes:

1. _____
2. _____
3. _____
4. _____
5. _____
6. _____
7. _____
8. _____
9. _____
10. _____
11. _____
12. _____
13. _____
14. _____
15. _____
16. _____
17. _____
18. _____
19. _____
20. _____
21. _____
22. _____
23. _____
24. _____
25. _____
26. _____

CHAPTER 4

BUILD YOUR OWN PLOT PLANNER

Plot Whisperer Tweet: *Everyday plotting: Show, don't tell, her emotional reaction by her actions, body language & words she speaks & what she neglects to say.*

A Plot Planner, as I said earlier, represents the structure of the Universal Story. Within the Universal Story certain events occur, each at their proper time. These events are marked within that story by what I have called Energetic Markers; these markers create a rhythm and balance to the Universal Story's structure. Once you understand that structure you have the freedom to do anything with your writing. The object of the exercises we're doing in this book is to line up the complete sequence of the story on a Plot Planner so that you can view the bigger picture of your story in its entirety.

The Beginning. The Middle. The End.

The beginning is one quarter of the entire story. In it, the protagonist has succumbed to boredom as expressed by a restlessness and dissatisfaction within her fixed world of daily routine and known facts. Finally, tension grows too great and she separates herself from her old existence in order to begin a journey toward an unknown world.

Stirred by an awakened desire—or even by blind greed—in the middle of a story the protagonist rushes toward immediate gratification of her desire. Yet as she does so, she quickly finds herself lost in the chaos and uncertainty of the unfamiliar. She is overwhelmed and fearful. Unwittingly, she moves nearer and nearer to self-discovery with a secret or unexpressed desire to reconnect and integrate with her lost other half.

In the end, now that the protagonist has awakened and activated her capacity for love and belonging, she sheds the grip of her former self. The story redeems all the challenges and discomfort, confusion, and fear and builds to a golden moment.

Within each of these three parts of a story—the beginning, the middle, and the end—sits one or more energetic markers. Four scenes in particular contain these markers; it's these scenes more than any others that control the energy of a story. Regardless of the specific form and content you give to these scenes, what is truly important is that the energy of the story rises and falls in ways to keep the reader and audience engaged all the way to the end of your book.

The Four Energetic Markers

Because these four scenes or moments in the Universal Story carry energetic surges that are powerful enough to turn the dramatic action of the story in a new direction, create a whole new level of intensity in the story, and contribute to its thematic significance, it's important, whenever possible, to identify these four energetic markers early in the writing process.

The rising and falling energy of the Universal Story marks the passage from birth to growth to death and rebirth. Every story has its own energy that operates within the universal pattern and contributes to the whole. The energetic markers guide you where and when to direct the flow of your scenes and how to encourage the energy to crest and fall for the greatest emotional impact. Knowledge of energetic markers in stories allows you to shape your story in the most compelling manner for the reader.

The scenes in the beginning quarter of the story have less conflict, tension, and suspense than do the scenes that come in the final quarter of the story. Think of your story as energy that rises to each of the energetic markers and falls after each of those turning points, only to rise again even higher at the next major scene.

Like signposts, energetic markers identify four major turning points in every story. Each energetic marker defines the dramatic action, characters, and thematic significance plot elements as your story energy expands and recedes.

First Energetic Marker: End of the Beginning

By the end of the beginning, the protagonist has appeared in varying situations. You, the writer, have presented her emotions to the reader by showing how she usually responds to the action around her.

The opening of the story introduces the core conflict of the narrative, which becomes the basis of the dramatic action—the protagonist wants something she thinks she either can or cannot have. Dramatic action calls for conflict, tension, suspense, and/or curiosity. The beginning introduces the reader to every thematic element through mood, tone, voice, word choices, metaphors and similes, and authentic details. The savvy reader knows on some level that these are important to the overall story. By the end of the first quarter of the story, the audience and readers are grounded in the here-and-now of the story world and all the elements of the climax have been foreshadowed.

As the first quarter of a story winds to a close, a scene or event symbolizes the moment when the protagonist separates from all that is familiar. Her sense of self is shaken. Her attachment to learned attitudes and behavior is severed. The energy surges and turns the story in a new direction, launching the protagonist into the actual story world itself with a goal that takes on greater meaning.

This moment occurs in Kathryn Stockett's *The Help* when Skeeter, the narrator, asks Aibileen to help her with her book. Though Aibileen refuses, simply by stating her intention to another person Skeeter shatters her old-world conventional roles and expectations. Her new life as a writer—and the real adventure—begins.

The first energetic marker signifies the end of the status quo. The scene launches the protagonist into the actual story world and signifies that there is no turning back.

Second Energetic Marker: Halfway Point

The second turning point, coming halfway through the story, forces the protagonist to willingly and consciously commit to the journey. After recommitting to her goal(s) at the halfway point of the Universal Story (or, in the case of the reluctant hero, committing for the first time), the protagonist feels the energy in her life turn and rise in significance. This energetic surge is a warning to the reader: Wake up. Be alert. A crisis is coming.

The recommitment scene lands somewhere around the halfway mark of your story.

In *The Help*, this point occurs when a third maid (of twelve needed) considers sharing her stories for Skeeter's book. This convinces Skeeter that she will successfully reach her goal. At the same time, Skeeter's friend rejects her, and that renews Skeeter's motivation to write the book.

Figure 6. Plot Planner—Energetic Markers
The Help, a novel by Kathryn Stockett and screenplay by Tate Taylor

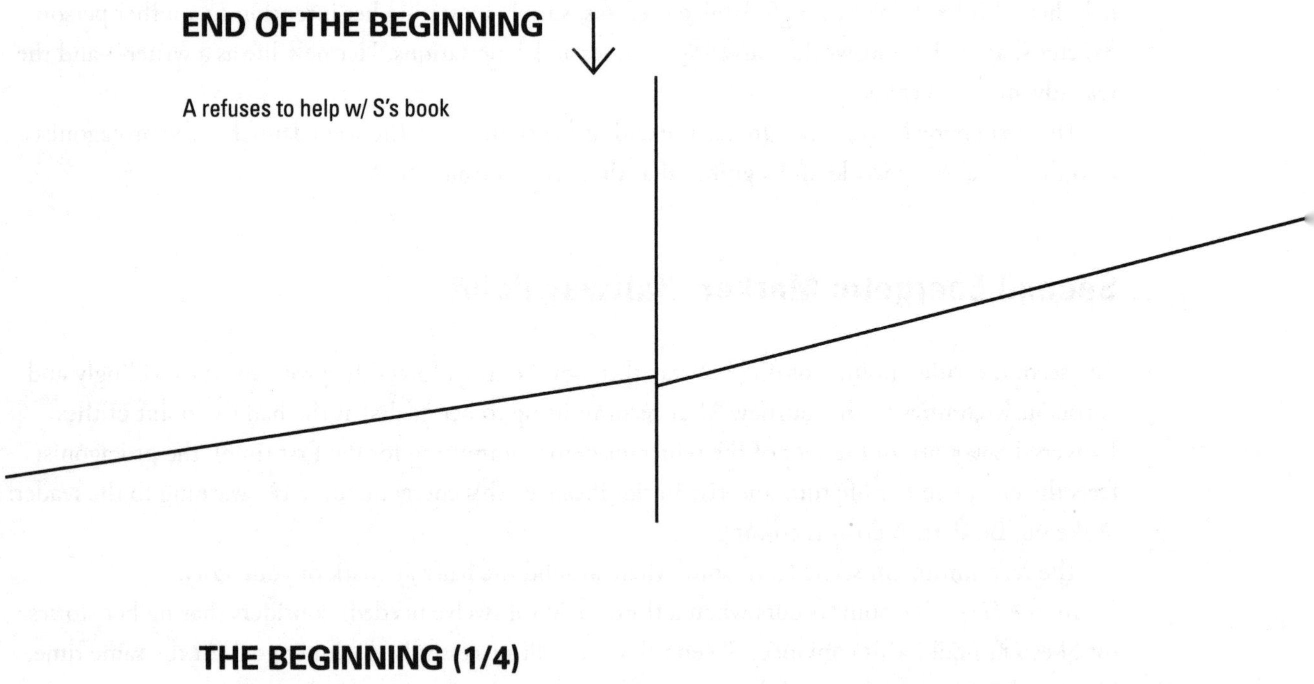

END OF THE BEGINNING ↓

A refuses to help w/ S's book

THE BEGINNING (1/4)

CLIMAX

↓

CRISIS

↓

S and A each stand up
separately to S's powerful
friend. A says goodbye to
the last children she will
help raise.

The Benefit; President Ken-
nedy is assassinated; S's mom
is dying; S learns the book must
be finished by year's end and
include a section about her maid.

S takes the NYC
literary assistant
job. A takes the
job at the local
newspaper.

↑

RECOMMITMENT SCENE

A third maid (of 12 needed) considers sharing
her stories for S's book. S's friend rejects her and
renews S's motivation to write the book.

↑

RESOLUTION

THE MIDDLE (1/2)   **THE END (1/4)**

Figure 7. Plot Planner—Energetic Markers
Major Pettigrew's Last Stand by Helen Simonson

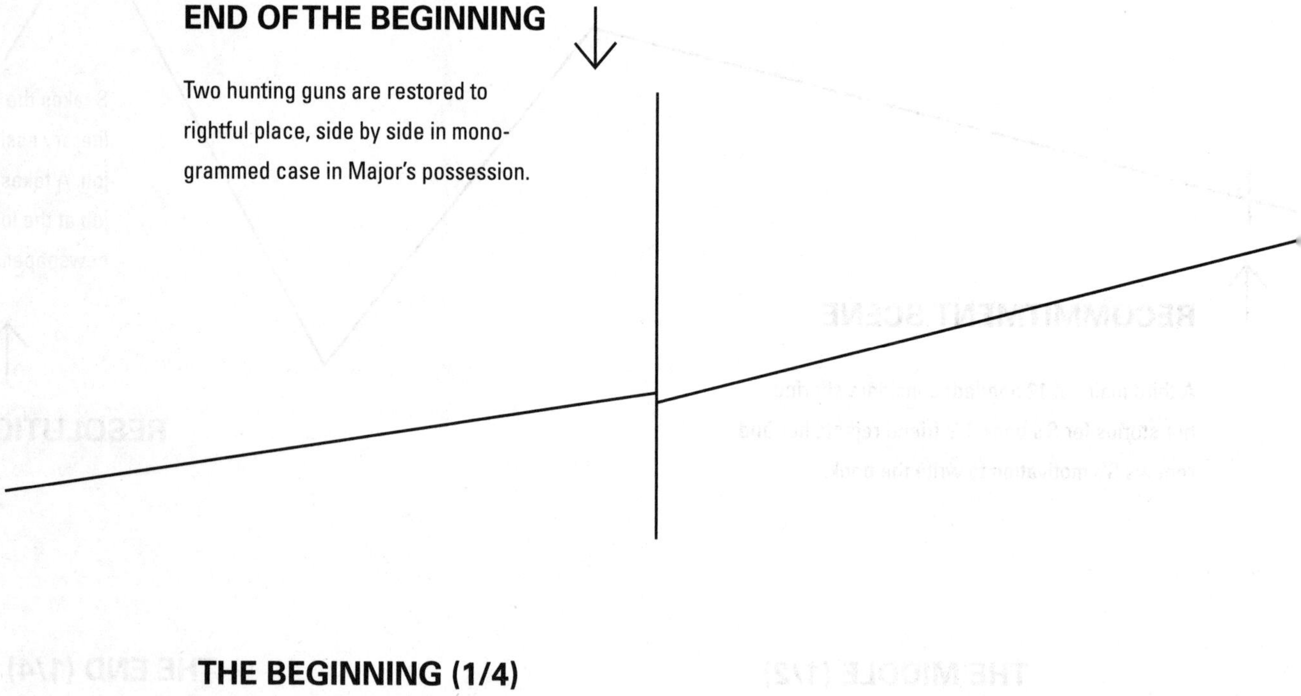

END OF THE BEGINNING

Two hunting guns are restored to rightful place, side by side in monogrammed case in Major's possession.

THE BEGINNING (1/4)

CLIMAX

↓

Major sacrifices one of the guns he had
once so coveted and faces death for the
woman he loves.

CRISIS

↓

"For the sake of these guns I let down
the woman I love in front of a whole
community of people." Mrs. Ali abruptly
quashes any chance for reconciliation.

He and Mrs. Ali marry.

↑

RESOLUTION

↑

RECOMMITMENT SCENE

The Major's forever dream comes true when
he is given the chance to show off the "famous
Pettigrew-Churchills" together to a small though
appreciative group of men.

THE MIDDLE (1/2)   **THE END (1/4)**

Third Energetic Marker: The Crisis

At nearly three-quarters of the way through the story, the energy rises to a new crest. The third energetic marker is the crisis, the greatest struggle of the entire story so far.

After surviving this ordeal toward the end of the middle of the story, the protagonist transmutes. But before the protagonist can transform, her old persona must, effectively, die. This is the role of the third energetic marker, the crisis.

Each scene in the middle portion of your story serves to march the protagonist step by step to the crisis. The energy builds until the volcano erupts.

The protagonist believes she is moving nearer and nearer to her long-term goal and consequent success. When the crisis hits, she is traumatized. The reader, however, has experienced the steady increase in the story's energy and feels the inevitability of this shocker from the linkage between each scene and from each thematic detail.

Toward the end of the middle of *The Help*, is a scene depicting the benefit. During this scene all the major characters are assembled and secrets are revealed and truths told. The day after, the energy breaks to a true crisis when Skeeter learns the book must be finished by the end of the year and include a section about Skeeter's maid.

Fourth Energetic Marker: The Climax

The fourth energetic marker holds the greatest intensity and highest drama in the entire story. It is called the climax.

At the climax, all the forces of the story come together for the final clash in which the protagonist directly confronts her major antagonist(s). Just when it looks as if all is permanently lost for the protagonist, she displays a rediscovered or refined awareness, skill, and/or knowledge. The climax is the crowning moment of the entire story, when the thematic significance of your story becomes clear to the reader.

The action by the protagonist answers the dramatic question posed at the beginning of the story: Will she or won't she be victorious? At the climax, all major conflicts are resolved. The energy of the entire story crescendoes at the climax and immediately is diffused.

Often in a plot consultation I find that the writer has summarized one or all of the energetic markers. It is tempting to gloss over writing the hard scenes. However, you can never skimp on the crucial scenes. The energetic markers must always be written in moment-to-moment action scenes.

The four energetic markers in each of the book examples we used in Chapter 1, 2, and 3 are reflected on the previous three Plot Planners.

Your Turn

In the following Plot Planner, fill in the four energetic markers for your novel, memoir, or screenplay.

After each notation, step back from the Plot Planner and consider where each scene falls in relationship to the entire story. View the end-of-the-beginning scene and the halfway-point scene in relationship to each other, the crisis to the climax, and the climax to the end-of-the-beginning scene.

Figure 8. Plot Planner—Energetic Markers
Esperanza Rising by Pam Munoz Ryan

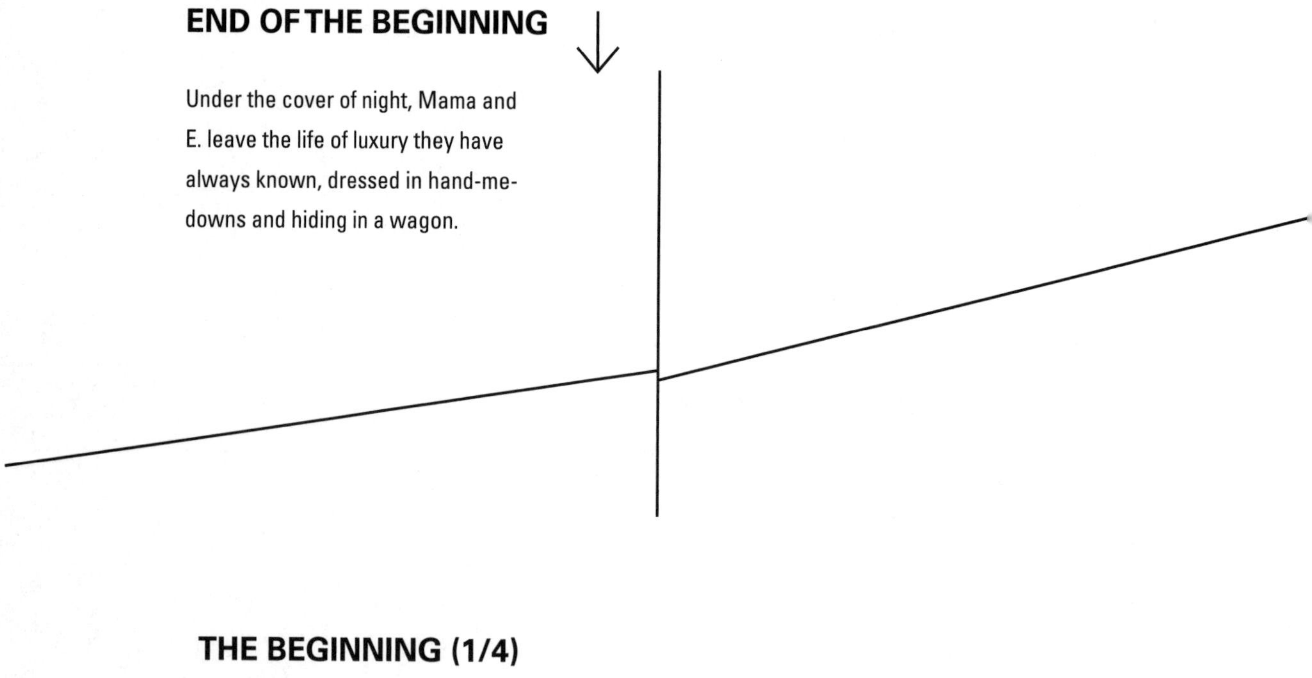

END OF THE BEGINNING

Under the cover of night, Mama and
E. leave the life of luxury they have
always known, dressed in hand-me-
downs and hiding in a wagon.

THE BEGINNING (1/4)

CLIMAX

↓

E. finishes knitting the
blanket.

CRISIS

↓

The workers go on
strike; E. and the others
are harassed; workers
are deported back to
Mexico; food runs out.

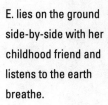

E. lies on the ground
side-by-side with her
childhood friend and
listens to the earth
breathe.

RECOMMITMENT SCENE

The church prayer E. recites no longer includes
returning to the past but includes prayers for those
in her new life in California.

↑

RESOLUTION

THE MIDDLE (1/2)   **THE END (1/4)**

Figure 9. Plot Planner—Energetic Markers

Working Title: _____

_____

Date: _____

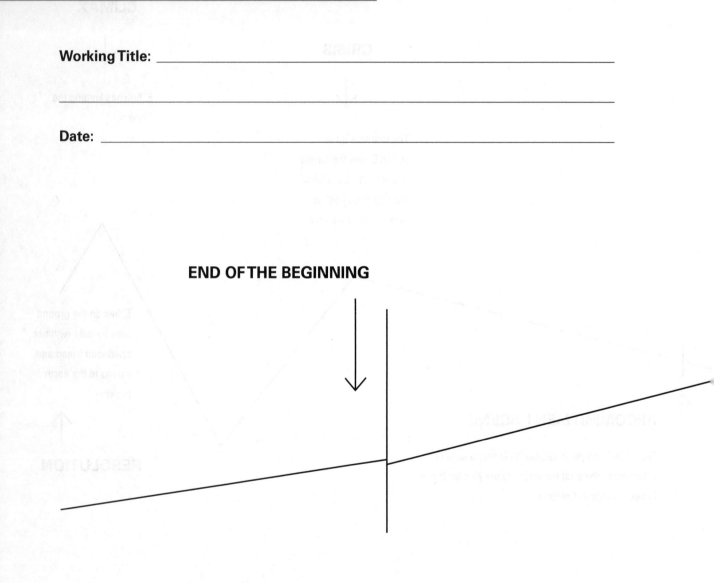

END OF THE BEGINNING

THE BEGINNING (1/4)

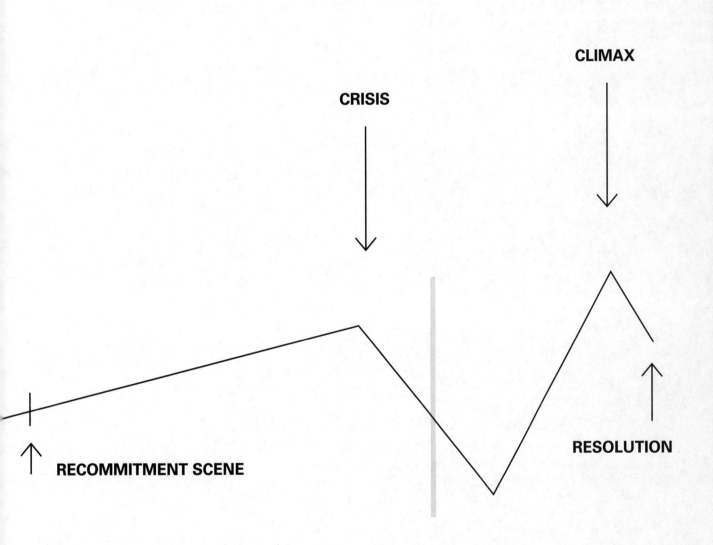

CLIMAX

CRISIS

RECOMMITMENT SCENE

RESOLUTION

THE MIDDLE (1/2)

THE END (1/4)

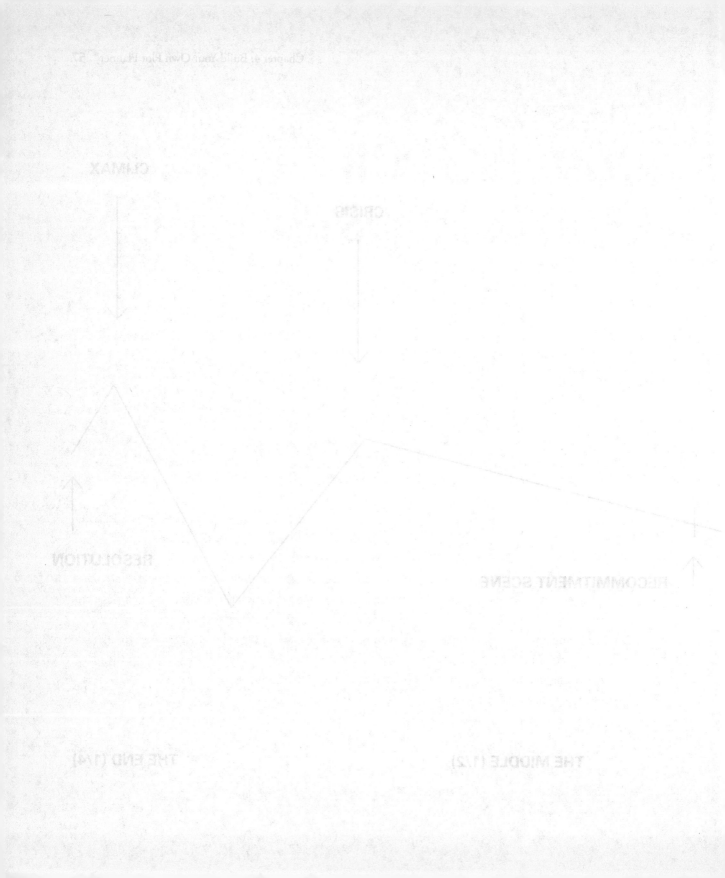

CHAPTER 5
WHO'S YOUR PROTAGONIST?

Plot Whisperer Tweet: *The Protagonist is often reactive in the Beginning and Middle of the story. At the End, she is completely proactive.*

Your characters' front story is determined by their goals and beliefs and traits. These are all the things you filled in on the character profiles in Chapter 2 of this workbook.

Behind each character's front story is a unique world made up of all her past experiences. In addition, every well-rounded and fully developed character has a backstory.

Some characters' backstories are banal, similar to everyone else's history. However, the character herself must always be unique. Hidden within her is the mystery of her individuality.

A character's backstory is everything that has happened to a character before she steps on stage and the actual story begins. Often the backstory includes an event that conveys trauma (physical or psychic), causing a backstory wound. Such a wound can happen at any age and at any point, diminishing the protagonist. Later, in Chapter 16, we'll explore the impact of a backstory wound on the plot.

In this chapter and in keeping with the parameters of the beginning, we'll cover the introductory elements of a character's backstory.

Who She Was Before

A character's backstory determines who she was before becoming who she is today in current story time. The character's backstory shapes her beliefs and expectations of life as well as her life direction.

In purely action-driven stories, the protagonist is often depicted as singular, as if birthed in isolation for the higher good, like Superman, the fictional comic book superhero; Ethan Hunt in the movie *Mission Impossible;* and Jack Ryan in Tom Clancy's novel *Clear and Present Danger.* In character-driven stories and virtually all women's fiction, the protagonist is emotionally affected by her past and the people who raised her.

Most of a story takes place as the protagonist engages with the outside world. The deeper impact of this action and what happens is registered inside the protagonist, causing either inner conflict or resulting in a reconciliation with the past.

Stories have the potential to change the reader. That potential is realized when the readers share in the emotional truth that results from a protagonist's grappling with her backstory. High-action violence, on the other hand, which does not show any emotional effects either on the protagonist or others, is a violation of the true human experience. Readers of such stories might be temporarily entertained, but they'll never participate in a deeper transformation that comes from reading a work of literature.

For an audience to connect to a story on an emotional level, they have to connect to the character. Today in movies, rather than a cardboard action figure enacting the action, we see three-dimensional characters, flaws and all. Characters with whom your readers identify broaden your market and lead to more readers.

GIVING BACKSTORIES

There is no need to give extended flashbacks or present backstories through memories of the past (unless the protagonist's backstory directly impacts the primary plot line, as do the following two examples). What is important about a character's backstory is *how the past is manifested at this moment in the scene as a thought, an emotion, a desire, a reaction, or an external event.* Such an impact is played out in the story's scenes. Whatever the reader and audience need to know about the protagonist emerges through the challenges she confronts in the scene on her way to her goal.

Early in *Major Pettigrew's Last Stand* by Helen Simonson, Mrs. Ali recounts a story from her background in the same detail in which it first happened:

"'I remember when I was a young girl, my father had this unshakable belief that the United Nations would evolve into a world government.' She shook her head and then raised her left hand from the wheel to waggle a finger at the windscreen. 'We will speak the languages of diplomacy and take our rightful places as world citizens,' she said, in a serious singsong. Then she sighed. 'He died still believing this, and my sister and I learned six languages between us to honor his memory.'"

This memory illustrates just how deeply her father's passion for change stirs in Mrs. Ali's heart. Major Pettigrew has his own memories, many of which are in direct opposition to Mrs. Ali's backstory beliefs. The major's memories thrive on his obsession with his father's final act, which the major has always judged as cowardice.

"It had been a midsummer day when his mother called him and Bertie into the dining room, where their father lay wasting away from emphysema in his rented hospital bed. The roses were very lush that year, and perfume from the nodding heads of an old pink damask came in at the open French doors . . . . His father, who was not as addled by his disease as everyone assumed, recognized the end. He sent for his two sons and his prized pair of Churchills."

The major knows what is coming next; he has been waiting for this moment nearly his entire life. Instead of keeping with tradition and passing both guns to the major, his father breaks up the pair, giving one gun to each son.

As the eldest son, the pair of hunting guns rightly belongs to the major. He lost what he most coveted because his father changed tradition in response to his love for both his sons. This backstory has left its imprint on Major in the beliefs he now, years later, holds dear:

"If there was one trait the Major despised in men, it was inconstancy. The habit of changing one's mind on a whim at the faintest breath of opposition; the taking up and putting down of hobbies, with the attendant bags of unused golf clubs in the garage and rusting weed trimmers leaning against sheds; the maneuverings of politicians in ways that sent uneven ripples of bother through the country. Such flailing about was anathema to the Major's send of order. Yet in the days following his excursion with Mrs. Ali and Grace, he found himself tempted to switch directions himself."

The more he exposes his heart and opens his feelings to Mrs. Ali, the more his deepest-held beliefs are challenged. Partway into the middle, long before his recommitment scene, the Major begins to long for life as it used to be before he took a fancy to Mrs. Ali.

ORDINARY BACKSTORY

A story—any story—is about a character transformed over time by the dramatic action. In order to make this character transformation more dramatic, the writer conveys in the beginning who and where the character is as dictated by her backstory before she is thrust into a new world.

Usually the protagonist has a life before the story begins, except for those stories that begin on or nearly at the protagonist's birth. (Even in such cases, the backstory may consist of the protagonist's family or circumstances.) The reader, in the first part of the story, gains a sense of the main character's framework of relationships and the degree to which she's governed by them. This gives the reader a starting point from which to evaluate the emotional change in the protagonist as the character is forced to break away and rely on herself in the middle of the story.

The customs, dogma, rules and regulations, values, and routines in the protagonist's early life come from outside the protagonist and often form a kind of inner protection for her. This includes everything from the foods she ate to the beliefs her parents instilled in her:

- "That is never right and just not done."
- "Men don't do that."
- "Women don't do that."
- "Our family never does that."
- "We're not that kind of people."

In the middle of the story when this protection is stripped away, the protagonist becomes vulnerable. If the reader knows the character's background, it's easier to gauge her degree of discomfort and pain as she pursues of her goal in the solitary, difficult, and dangerous new world of the middle and the end.

Stay Open to New Ideas

As ideas for your characters' backstories flood your imagination, try lots of different lives for your characters until you find what works best for the story. Being too set on your path too early in the process of writing a story can lead you in the wrong direction and can be sadly limiting. That said, some stories come fully formed to the writer from the start.

There are many unexpected experiences available to your protagonist, and it's best to keep your mind open to them. Yes, you should plot carefully, but some of the best scenes aren't planned. As you work on your story, evaluate the unexpected things that jump in your path and surprise you about your protagonist. The trick is to keep a healthy balance between exploration and pre-plot expectations.

HOW TO SHOW BACKSTORY

As I said earlier, you must show a character's backstory through the actions she takes in the front story.

Often, the most powerful means of telling a character's backstory is through showing how and through what she now derives her sense of identity based on her backstory. The less the writer tells the actual details of the backstory, the more the reader participates in the story, as she is required through her own imagination to fill in the missing blanks with the hints you provide.

Your Turn

Develop a backstory for your protagonist. If you identified more than one main character in your story, carefully consider how many characters you'll develop with an in-depth backstory. Too many backstories can bog a story down.

Photocopy the following Backstory Chart for as many major characters as appear in your story. Then fill it out—one chart for each story. Once you've completed this exercise, lay the backstory charts side by side in front of you. Read them through carefully, and fill out the Backstory Evaluation Chart. This will help you judge how these backstories fit together and balance one another.

Backstory Chart

Backstory for (character's name): _____

Place of birth: _____

Sex: _____

Parents: _____

Siblings: _____

Education: _____

Health: _____

Marital status: _____

Backstory Evaluation Chart

How are these various backstories similar? _____

_____

_____

How are they different? _____

_____

_____

What thematically ties the backstories together? _____

_____

_____

Backstory Memories

Write three short sketches (150–300 words each) about the protagonist's memories of her life in nearly the detail in which it first happened. One sketch may be about something sweet or poignant or that worked out the way she hoped it would and how that success shapes her beliefs today. Another sketch can deal with something that worked out differently that she hoped it would, resulting in failure or disappointment or trauma that shapes her beliefs today.

Include as much detail as you like and write as much or as little of your character's backstory as you feel is necessary.

Sketch No. 1

_____

_____

_____

_____

_____

_____

_____

_____

_____

Sketch No. 2

_____

_____

_____

_____

_____

_____

_____

_____

_____

Sketch No. 3

_____

_____

_____

_____

_____

_____

_____

_____

_____

PART II

Begin Plotting

CHAPTER 6

CREATE AN INTRODUCTION CHECKLIST

Plot Whisperer Tweet: *Restraint in the beginning leads to a great impact at both the crisis and the climax.*

The beginning generally spans the first quarter of a complete story. It serves as an archetypal force to accomplish one specific role—invite change.

Archetypal forces are patterns or the mythic original on which a pattern is based. The pattern of the Universal Story works so well because it catches readers' imaginations and sets off vibrations deep in our collective consciousness. We feel the pattern in life calling all around us, warning us and inspiring us. We want to hear it again and again. Each time the archetypal energy of the Universal Story repeats itself, rather than wear out with age it creates recognition and connections through the power of repetition.

Some beginnings happen quickly; the right direction toward change is assured. In other story beginnings, the grip of the past is slow to reveal a new opening forward to change.

Beginnings seduce the protagonist with promises of something new and different for the sole purpose of pulling her out of where she is at the beginning of the story, both literally and figuratively, into the unknown of the middle.

Details and action at the beginning of a story serve as stark contrast to the details and action that follow in the middle. The more different the beginning is to what happens in the middle, the greater the effect of the contrast.

Contract with Your Readers

The story's time and setting are introduced in the beginning: This part of the story sets up the dramatic action and underlying conflict; you introduce all the major characters, giving the reader an idea of who they are, their emotional makeup, and the weight they carry in the story. You allude to the theme and introduce the protagonist's short-term goal. You also give at least a sense of the protagonist's long-term goal.

Each of these beginning elements serve to establish a contract with your readers. You tell them what your story is going to be about (as well as what it's not going to be about) and extend them a promise of the tone of the story—whether it will be romantic, full of action and adventure, quiet, noisy, and so forth.

The Da Vinci Code by Dan Brown begins by immediately orienting the reader. Brown establishes who: Robert Langdon, a professor of religious symbology at Harvard University. He tells us where: Hotel Ritz Paris. Finally, he tells the reader what: Someone is dead, and the Judicial Police are involved. This is all in the first two or three pages. Thus begins both the character emotional development plot line and the dramatic action plot line.

Next Brown introduces the murderer, Silas, and establishes that "the stakes [in the killing] were incalculable." Next enters police captain Fache, a determined and "angry ox." Finally, we find out that an ultraconservative secret society of the Catholic Church is involved and that cryptography will play a part in the story. Both these elements tie Langdon's private passions to a bigger, more universal public subject, and thus the thematic plot line is launched.

By this point, we are dead center in the beginning of Brown's story. In the introductory phase of the beginning of *The Da Vinci Code*, Brown keeps the reader's attention by giving only enough information to whet the imagination. He finishes every single scene with a cliffhanger.

Almost halfway through the beginning, when Brown introduces the police cryptography expert Sophie, the stakes in the story rise. There to help Langdon on his journey, Sophie ups the ante by challenging him to run away with her (escaping Fache, who thinks Langdon is involved in the murder). Langdon's jump from the window acts as a mini-crisis that occurs toward the end of the middle of the first quarter of the story (at just the spot where the crisis will hit in the bigger story—toward the end of the middle).

When we find that Langdon and Sophie did not in fact jump out the window of the Louvre, the stakes rise ever higher. Brown ends the beginning or the first quarter of the book with one *big* scene and five shorter, but equally significant, scenes.

First the big scene: This is where Sophie first learns of the keystone—literally the key to the next part of the plot. In the following few short scenes, Brown unrolls further plot elements: Sophie learns of the pagan goddess worship cult, Langdon fully commits to the adventure, Silas is identified as a killer, and Fache connects Sophie to Langdon.

The story is now set up, with suspense and tension and conflict in every scene. We know almost all the characters and what is at stake. If, at this point in the story, the reader commits to your book, she'll read it to the end.

Pick up a book you couldn't put down until the end and see if it doesn't follow a similar narrative pattern in the first quarter of the story.

Contrast and Foreshadowing

Every beginning uses certain techniques to draw the reader in further. Among the most important of these are contrast and foreshadowing, which work in tandem throughout the beginning of a story. Every element introduced in the beginning provides a contrast for the middle and serves to foreshadow what comes later. Foreshadowing is like planting seeds that quietly and irreversibly germinate, always with a glimpse of the ending to come.

Introduction Checklist

When reviewing the beginning of your plot, run down the following checklist to make sure you've included all these elements.

SETTING
The setting of a story is home to the life the character lives now. It tells a lot about her. Stories that begin with a young protagonist—though she does not always have a say in where and how her life plays out—show how she interacts within her current setting and impacts how she is perceived by the reader. As she matures, the protagonist makes choices. The effects of those choices are reflected in changes within the setting or, occasionally, the creation of an entirely new setting.

Settings have a hand in molding the characters. Every element of a character's external appearance opens a window for the reader to see into who she is now. Settings show the rhythm of her mind and the sensitivities of her heart.

A character's choices and afflictions and circumstances in and about her setting represent her and the broader meaning of the story itself.

In *Faithful Place* by Tana French, the mystery of a missing suitcase brings Detective Frank of the Dublin Undercover squad face-to-face with his past (backstory wound). The story begins with the description of a setting so pivotal to the character's transformation that each time the actual location is mentioned and every single time the protagonist is thrust into that setting, the process of transmutation continues.

In this story, that place of high energy and testing is Number 16 at the top of Faithful Place, "littered with beer cans and fag ends and lost virginities."

Chapter 1 is set on a "Friday afternoon in the beginning of December" at the house in which Detective Frank used to live with his wife and daughter. In contrast to the setting he grew up in, her place is "jaw-droppingly tasteful semi-d on a manicured cul-de-sac in Dalkey." The rest of the beginning of *Faithful Place* takes place at Faithful Place. What begins as a broad view of the neighborhood narrows to his parent's house and all the way back to Number 16 and the room at the top and . . . the basement.

The stark contrast between the life of Frank's past and his failed married life shows just how distant Frank has grown from his past and leads the reader to surmise that in order for Frank to move on in his life, he must first make peace with this bit of his past.

The setting at the beginning of a story foreshadows what comes in the middle and especially at the end in Number 16, Faithful Place.

Settings create the mood of the scene and, in the beginning of a story, foreshadow the mood to come. A dark setting among towering mountains and skyscrapers creates a brooding atmosphere. A lakefront of light sets a warm and imaginative mood. Plant clues in the setting here at the beginning of the story about the changes to come. Add doubt and darkness or hint at the longing and light to come.

Whatever the mood and wherever the location, the setting is where the action of the story takes place.

THEME

Themes define what your story is about. Themes are shown through symbols, metaphors and similes, and mood and setting. A story begins with hints about the story's theme.

In her novel *A Thousand Acres*, Jane Smiley rethinks King Lear. Her story is set in a different time and place but deals with the same themes of greed, gratitude, miscalculations, betrayal, and love.

If you are just beginning to imagine your story, keep an eye open for the themes that arise in the scenes you create. Themes of responsibility, regret, cognition, perception, trauma, loss, disintegration, death, adaptation, intuition, life, or peace help to lay the groundwork toward meaning and foreshadow the contrast ahead.

PROTAGONIST

The protagonist is changed or transformed over the course of a story by the dramatic action. Who the character is at the beginning of the story is not the same character she will be at the end. This change or transformation in the character reflects the impact of the story's dramatic action.

Action intertwines with the character emotional development. The protagonist's character traits are introduced at the beginning of the story. Throughout the narrative, the action drives the ultimate transformation the character undergoes. Although the character in the introductory chapters may seem static, it's important to introduce her character goals that will be resolved in the story. The fears, flaws, prejudices, or strengths she must overcome or develop are introduced in the beginning to contrast with and foreshadow the necessary skills and knowledge and abilities she needs for the climax at the end.

An old axiom teaches that all energy follows thought. Where the protagonist puts her thoughts is where the energy of the story goes. Part of the character's ultimate transformation at the end comes from a change in her thought patterns, in what the protagonist believes about life, and what she wants now.

SECONDARY CHARACTERS

Secondary characters reflect lessons the protagonist needs to learn and the abilities she will need to prevail at the end. A secondary character often reflects the natural and hidden abilities in the protagonist. They mirror potentials within the protagonist, potentialities she has forgotten or lost or was robbed of.

Your Turn

Fill in the following Introduction Checklist for the beginning of your story. As you complete this exercise, keep in mind how the plot elements addressed in the beginning of your story contrast and foreshadow plot elements to come in the middle.

1. If you are at the imaginative phase of writing a story, start by imagining the answers to the following list.
2. If you are at the generative stage, use the beginning elements as prompts for your early drafts.
3. At the refinement stage of completing your novel, memoir, or screenplay, review how these elements play out in every scene at the beginning of the book.

Introduction Checklist

SETTING

Describe in a couple of sentences the setting at the beginning of your story.

_____

_____

_____

What does the setting say about the protagonist?

_____

_____

_____

_____

What does the setting represent and convey about her choices and afflictions and circumstances?

_____

_____

_____

_____

What main action takes place at this setting?

_____

_____

_____

How does the setting at the beginning contrast with and foreshadow what comes in the middle and at the end?

_____

_____

_____

THEMES

List the themes introduced at the beginning of your story:

_____

_____

_____

List the symbols, metaphors, and similes used to convey the themes listed previously.

How do these beginning symbols, metaphors, and similes contrast and foreshadow what comes in the middle and at the end?

_____

_____

_____

What mood will this setting instill in the reader?

_____

_____

_____

How does the mood at the beginning contrast with and/or foreshadow the exotic setting and mood coming in the story?

_____

_____

_____

PROTAGONIST

Name:

_____

Which trait(s) of the character directly impacts the course of the action in the story (both positively and negatively) and are introduced at the beginning?

_____

_____

_____

How do the character's fears, flaws, prejudices, and strengths now at the start of the story contrast with her fears, flaws, prejudices, and strengths at the end of the story?

_____

_____

_____

_____

_____

Which of the necessary skills, knowledge, and abilities she needs for success at the climax are missing at the beginning?

_____

_____

_____

What flaws or fears in the beginning foreshadow and contribute to her crisis in the middle?

_____

_____

_____

What did/does the protagonist want just before the story begins?

_____

_____

What does the character do in the beginning?

_____

_____

Why is she doing it?

_____

_____

How does that contrast and foreshadow what she does at the end?

_____

_____

Why?

_____

_____

How do her goals propel the story forward in the beginning?

_____

_____

How do her goals define the story's dramatic action plot?

_____

_____

What thoughts preoccupy your protagonist's mind at the beginning of the story?

_____

_____

_____

Where do those thoughts send the energy of the story?

_____

_____

_____

What does the protagonist believe about life that affects what she wants now at the beginning of the story?

_____

_____

What does the protagonist believe the successful attainment of her goal will bring her beyond the actual goal itself?

_____

_____

SECONDARY CHARACTERS

List the major secondary characters:

_____

_____

_____

_____

_____

What aspect(s) of the protagonist do the secondary characters reflect at the beginning of your story?

_____

_____

What lessons do the secondary characters have that reflect what the protagonist needs to learn to prevail at that climax?

_____

_____

What abilities do the secondary characters have that mirror the abilities the protagonist can most easily develop and use on her way to achieve success?

_____

_____

How do the secondary characters foreshadow in the beginning the upcoming story events and action that follow?

_____

_____

How does what the secondary characters represent at the beginning of the story contrast to what they represent at the end?

_____

_____

How does what the secondary characters want conflict with what the protagonist wants?

_____

_____

Notes to Self

_____

_____

_____

_____

_____

_____

_____

_____

_____

_____

_____

_____

_____

CHAPTER 7
BUILD THE OPENING SCENES

Plot Whisperer Tweet: *In great stories, the dramatic action transforms the protagonist. This transformation makes a story meaningful.*

Stories come alive through action. At every stage of writing and reading a story, the narrative longs for the intimacy created in moment-by-moment scenes. A scene is the sensuous core structure of a story. Understand scene and you'll have discovered the essence of plot.

You have imagined where your story takes place, who the major characters are and what they want, and you have at least a glimmer of where they will be at the end of the story. Next, expand those ideas into scenes. Generate the first quarter scenes for your novel, memoir, or screenplay with the help of the Scene Tracker.

A Scene Tracker peels apart the different layers of plot and allows for a close-up picture of your story. Use the Scene Tracker to create and analyze the scenes of your story.

Guide to Using a Scene Tracker

A Scene Tracker is the place to keep track of all the threads of the character emotional development plot, the dramatic action plot, and thematic significance plot, and points to how to deepen and expand every scene.

After you have generated and written many more scenes in the first draft of your story than needed, for any story, a Scene Tracker can show you which scenes to keep and which ones to cut.

Filling out a Scene Tracker is not writing a story. Writing words is. However, filling out a Scene Tracker supports writing the words of your story.

The Seven Essential Elements of Scene

Whether you write short stories, novels, or memoirs and/or creative nonfiction, you will write countless scenes. Keep in mind the following elements when creating a scene. Just as plot has many different layers, every scene has layers of functions, too.

1. The first layer of every scene deals with time and setting. Often this layer is implied or understood from the scenes and summaries that precede it. Time and setting is crafted to ground readers in the "where" and "when" of the scene.

2. Dramatic action that unfolds moment by moment on the page makes up the next layer of scene.

3. Embedded within layer two is a layer of conflict, tension, and/or suspense. The conflict does not have to be overt, but it must be present in some form. For a real page-turner, fill a scene with tension or suspense or something unknown lurking in the shadows. Setbacks and failure create suspense, conflict, and tension, unlike success and good news, which don't.

4. Conflict, tension, and suspense drive the reader to turn the page. The character's emotional development—the heart of the story—motivates that action. Readers read stories to learn about a character's emotional development. The word "development" implies growth or change. Therefore, character becomes a layer. The change or emotional development at the core of character is yet another.

5. The protagonist hopes to accomplish a specific goal within the scene. Every scene where the character's goal is clearly understood creates a question for the reader:
   Will she be successful . . . or not?

6. Most stories revolve around a protagonist who goes after something, fails, and tries again. Each time life sends your protagonist reeling, she struggles to her feet and tries anew. Since at this point in the story it is best if the protagonist is in worse shape when she ends the scene than when she starts it, bear in mind that no matter how bad things get for the character, they can always get worse.

Change is essential to keep your reader's interest. A character and her emotional state should be constantly changing. If you write a scene where this is missing, chances are that the scene will fall flat and turn your story stagnant. The emotional change the character experiences within each scene does not have to be monumental, but she does have to feel and experience some sort of emotional reaction to the dramatic action in the scene. If not, you've done nothing to develop the character, which raises the question: why not?

For example, in the first scene of *The Sea-Wolf* by Jack London, Humphrey van Weyden, the protagonist, begins the book in a positive state; he is traveling on a ferryboat from San Francisco to Sausalito confident and eager to work on a projected essay he has thought of calling "The Necessity of Freedom: A Plea for the Artist." Some paragraphs later, in the same scene, a red-faced stranger appears. (This is a clever technique for creating tension and suspense because a stranger inevitably evokes curiosity in the reader. Who is this person? A messenger of doom, an antagonist? Or an agent of reward, an ally?) The stranger hints to van Weyden that because of all the fog in the San Francisco Bay, things are amiss. Soon after, the ferry bearing the two men crashes into another vessel. As chaos ensues, fear grips van Weyden. Thus, he ends the scene in worse shape than he was at the beginning.

7. Thematic significance creates the final layer of scene and the overall spirit of your story. The key to the theme lies in your reasons for writing the story and what you want your readers to take away from it. When the details you use in the scene support the thematic significance, you have created an intricately layered scene that provides meaning and depth to the overall plot.

Here is an analysis, done with the Scene Tracker, of the opening scenes of F. Scott Fitzgerald's *The Great Gatsby*. Note that in each scene we look for details that bring out the overall theme of the book.
Section: The Beginning (1/4)
Notes: Thematic Significance: Fascination with wealth and another man's wife and old dreams is self-destructive.

Chapter/ Scene	Date and Setting	Character Emotional Development	Goal	Dramatic Action Plot	Conflict	Emotional Change	Thematic Significance / Details
Ch. 1, Scene 1	1924 summer; Long Island; East Egg	**Nick** late 20s; from college went to army & now beginning business life; has girlfriend in Chicago	To have dinner with Daisy and Tom	Tour of the estate	X	-/--/-	"Two young women . . . buoyed up as though upon an anchored balloon" (shows insubstantiality & inner emptiness)
		Tom married to Daisy; enormously wealthy family; football player in college; "a cruel body"	Tom's "scientific stuff" indicates his concern for preserving status quo which foreshadows Gatsby's threat				
		Daisy second cousin once removed; "absurd, charming little laugh"; "low, thrilling voice"; lonely since moving from Chicago; two-year-old daughter; needs others to decide for her					
		Jordan Baker famous golfer					
Scene 2	same night, same place	**Daisy** hopes her daughter will be "The best thing a girl can be in this world, a beautiful little fool."		Nick learns of Tom's infidelities	X	+/-	Introduces theme of adultery
		Jordan tells Nick, "Tom's got some woman in New York."					
Scene 3	same night, West Egg	**Gatsby** Intro Gatsby, who lives next door	Go home to West Egg	Gatsby is trembling	X	+/-	Gatsby's house is pretentious; imitation of European structure; the color is green
Ch. 2, Scene 1	halfway between West Egg & NYC	**Tom** Introduces Wilson & mistress to Nick	Going to NY with Tom	Husband is present as Tom and mistress flirt	X	-/--	Valley of Ashes; Landscape with waste produced by manufacture of wealth; gigantic, sightless eyes; dust on Ford and ashen veil on hair

The Major Elements of a Beginning Set of Scenes

THE BEGINNING ENDS

The beginning ends when the protagonist's domesticated and safe world causes her to suffer and she no longer belongs there. False and lost, she is squeezed out of the confinement of the past. The energy of the story twists in a new direction when she enters a new beginning pure again and ready for change at the middle. What comes in the middle is new and different. Because it is beyond imitation and limitation, it is also dangerous.

First . . . the beginning ends.

Your Turn

Follow the general structure of the Scene Tracker for *The Great Gatsby* shown previously. As you begin tracking your scenes for the beginning quarter of your story, refer back to the transformational ideas you generated in Chapter 1 and the character profiles from Chapter 2. Use the partial scene list you started in Chapter 3 as well as the scenes at each of the Energetic Markers as plotted on your mini-Plot Planner in Chapter 4.

Track all beginning scenes up to and including the first energetic marker. Anchor the last scene on the last line of the last Scene Tracker template in the chapter with the End of the Beginning scene you generated in Chapter 4.

Project Name:

Date:

Draft:

SCENE TRACKER

Chapter:

Scene/ Summary	Dates/Setting	Character Emotional Development	Goal
SCENE 1			
SCENE 2			
SCENE 3			
OPTIONAL			
OPTIONAL			

Notes:

Dramatic/ Action Plot	Conflict	Emotional Change	Thematic Significance/Details

Figure 2. Scene Tracker Template
Copyright © 2004, Martha Alderson

Project Name:

Date:

Draft:

SCENE TRACKER

Chapter:

Scene/ Summary	Dates/Setting	Character Emotional Development	Goal
SCENE 1			
SCENE 2			
SCENE 3			
OPTIONAL			
OPTIONAL			

Notes:

Dramatic/ Action Plot	Conflict	Emotional Change	Thematic Significance/Details

Figure 2. Scene Tracker Template
Copyright © 2004, Martha Alderson

Project Name:

Date:

Draft:

SCENE TRACKER

Chapter:

Scene/ Summary	Dates/Setting	Character Emotional Development	Goal
SCENE 1			
SCENE 2			
SCENE 3			
OPTIONAL			
OPTIONAL			

Notes:

Dramatic/ Action Plot	Conflict	Emotional Change	Thematic Significance/Details

Figure 2. Scene Tracker Template
Copyright © 2004, Martha Alderson

Project Name:

Date:

Draft:

SCENE TRACKER

Chapter:

Scene/ Summary	Dates/Setting	Character Emotional Development	Goal
SCENE 1			
SCENE 2			
SCENE 3			
OPTIONAL			
OPTIONAL			

Notes:

Dramatic/ Action Plot	Conflict	Emotional Change	Thematic Significance/Details

CHAPTER 8

BEGIN AT THE BEGINNING

Plot Whisperer Tweet: *Character Emotional Development is cumulative, based on all the scenes over time, is long-term & transformative.*

The Universal Story is a continuity of stories that span tens of thousands of years. It continues to unfold around us, embedding its features in our minds and souls.

As we've seen, the line of the Plot Planner follows the path of the Universal Story. A Plot Planner shows you the underlying structure of your story at a higher level than the words with which you write. Create a Plot Planner at every stage of writing your novel, memoir, and screenplay.

The Advanced Plot Planner

At the imaginative stage, the Plot Planner is a bold expression of a story's broad possibilities. During the generative stage, the visual representation of your story becomes a record of progress. At the refinement stage, a Plot Planner serves as an analytical tool.

Whereas the Scene Tracker deals with individual sensory elements in individual scenes, a Plot Planner shows how all the scenes flow together as a whole at the overall story level.

Figure 10. Plot Planner for the Beginning of *The Hours* Screenplay by David Hare, based on the novel of the same name by Michael Cunningham.

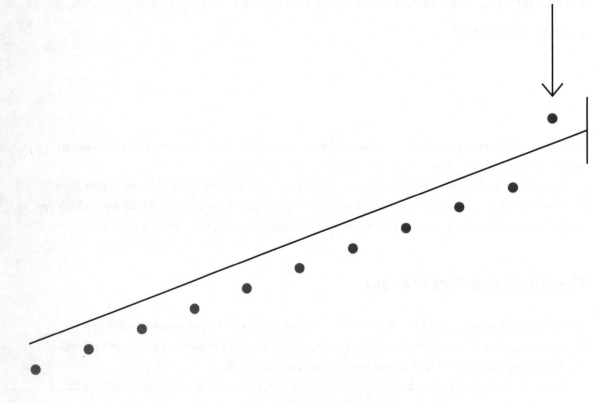

END OF THE BEGINNING

THE BEGINNING (1/4)

Figure 11. Plot Planner for the Beginning of *The Da Vinci Code* by Dan Brown

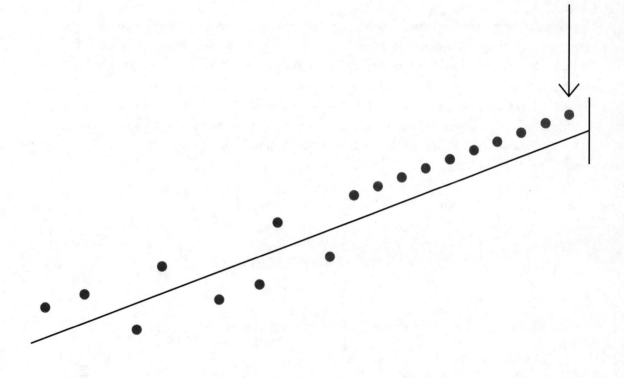

END OF THE BEGINNING

THE BEGINNING (1/4)

The Plot Planners on the previous pages show how the energy flows at the beginning of two different stories. The scenes are marked with a dot. For now, simply view the rhythm produced by the way the scenes flow together.

Match each story with a category.

1. A story with rapid-fire intensity shoots all the scenes above the line.
2. Slower and more internal stories snake their way up and down the Plot Planner line to the end of the beginning.

Above and Below the Line

Imagine a story as a conflict between energies of light and dark. The energy shifts back and forth between the protagonist and the antagonists of the story. The antagonists represent darkness as they strive to keep the protagonist as she currently exists. The protagonist represents the light in the struggle to evolve. Change is never easy, and a protagonist bound in the darkness of her backstory and locked in repetitive patterns dictated by her flaw will necessarily be in for a rough time.

Scenes where the internal forces (the character herself) and external forces (antagonists) push against the protagonist are plotted above the Plot Planner line. These are scenes of:

loss   unhappiness
failing to cope   flaws
grief   hatred
rebellion   loss of power
ambition   anger

and filled with   catastrophe
discovery   a chase
conflict   betrayal
tension   deception
suspense   curiosity

The stronger the internal and external forces are that oppose the protagonist, the more dramatic the action scenes.

An intense dramatic action scene often calls for a lull in the action afterward. These below-the-line scenes are a time to show the impact of the confrontation on both the antagonist and the protagonist, and the shift in the latter's direction toward her goal. When the protagonist pushes toward her desire, she directs the energy. Scenes that break the intensity of the sequence upward and show her feeling include:

calm and coping	contemplative
planning	in control
solving problems	

These are plotted beneath the Plot Planner line. (Refer to Figure 1 for an idea of which scenes belong above and which ones go below the Plot Planner line.)

A protagonist who wants something enough to take action against all the antagonists within and without creates a story.

The End of the Beginning Scene

The scenes build from the beginning to the end of life as the protagonist currently knows it. The story beginning ends when the grip of some long-enduring rigid mentality loosens; at that moment the story shifts from the beginning into the middle. In *State of Wonder* by Ann Patchett, the protagonist leaves the beginning when she locates the threshold guardians and penetrates into the depths of the Amazon River basin; in *The Alchemist* by Paulo Coelho, the protagonist loses all his money and leaves the beginning to enter the exotic world with only two small stones; in the middle-grade novel *Stargirl,* by Jerry Spinelli, the protagonist leaves the beginning for the exotic world in the middle when she crosses from her team's side of the basketball court to cheer the rival team.

Throughout the beginning of the romance novel *Candle in the Window* by Christina Dodd, Lady Saura keeps her blindness a secret from Sir William of Miravel, who has been temporarily blinded. All that changes when he regains his eyesight. The beginning ends. Both she and he are forced into the exotic world of the middle where now only one of them is blind.

Figure 12. Plot Planner for the Beginning of *Candle in the Window*

Lady Saura = S.
Sir William = W.

Introduced in the Beginning:

- All the major characters, including the dog
- Abuse Lady Saura has suffered by her stepfather
- Love story subplot for Maud and Lord Peter (intro in Ch. 1)

KEY:

(CED): Character Emotional Development
(DA): Dramatic Action
(TS): Thematic Significance

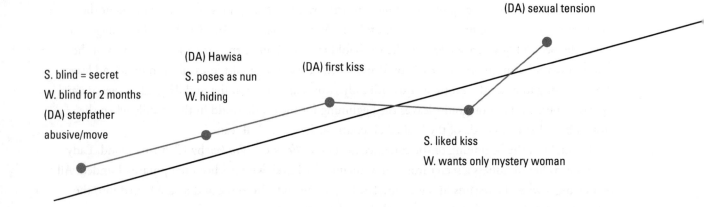

(DA) sexual tension

(DA) Hawisa
S. poses as nun
W. hiding

(DA) first kiss

S. blind = secret
W. blind for 2 months
(DA) stepfather
abusive/move

S. liked kiss
W. wants only mystery woman

THE BEGINNING (1/4)

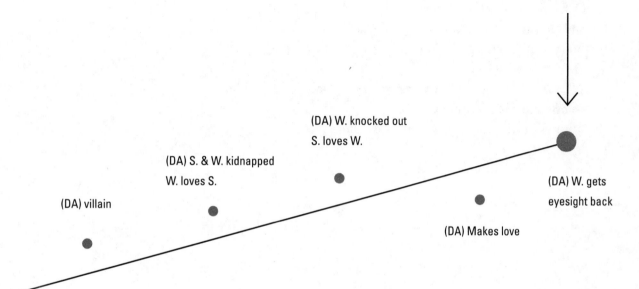

END OF THE BEGINNING

(DA) W. knocked out
S. loves W.

(DA) S. & W. kidnapped
W. loves S.

(DA) villain

(DA) W. gets
eyesight back

(DA) Makes love

Character Profile for Lady Saura

Overall Story Goal: To find a man who accepts her for who she is

Stands in Her Way: Her belief that she is nothing because of her blindness

What Does She Stand to Lose: All chances of happiness

Flaw: Does not trust herself or men

Strength: Competent/Beautiful/Heart of a lion/Brave/Intelligent

Hates: Pity

Loves: Being in charge

Fears: Not being worthy

Secret: Blind

The End of the Beginning Checklist

Just as we made a checklist for the introductory scenes, we need one for the transition from the beginning to the middle of the story. Here's an example from the novel I just mentioned, *Candle in the Window*.

1. One-sentence description of the End of the Beginning scene:
   Sir William of Miravel gets his eyesight back
2. What does the protagonist leave behind?
   The feeling of equality
3. What is interfering with her moving into the middle of the story?
   Being blind while he can see
4. What gift enables her to move into the middle?

Lady Saura loves Sir William

Your Turn

First, before you create a Plot Planner for the beginning of your story, double-check the scene you have imagined or written for the End of the Beginning. Check off and answer each of the following questions about the End of the Beginning scene.

Checklist for the End of the Beginning Scene

1. One-sentence description of the End of the Beginning scene:

    _____

2. What does the protagonist leave behind?

    _____

3. What is interfering with her moving into the middle of the story?

    _____

4. What gift enables her to move into the middle?

    _____

Now, plot your beginning scenes on the Plot Planner provided. Condense the elements for the beginning scenes you generated on the Scene Tracker in the last chapter into one word or phrase. Print the phrase on a mini-sticky note. In order, place each scene above or below the Plot Planner line for the beginning of your story.

If you marked an "X" under the conflict column of the Scene Tracker, place the scene above the line of the Plot Planner.

If there is no "X" in the conflict column of the Scene Tracker, put the scene below the Plot Planner line.

Figure 13. Plot Planner for the Beginning

Working Title: _____

_____

Date: _____

THE BEGINNING (1/4)

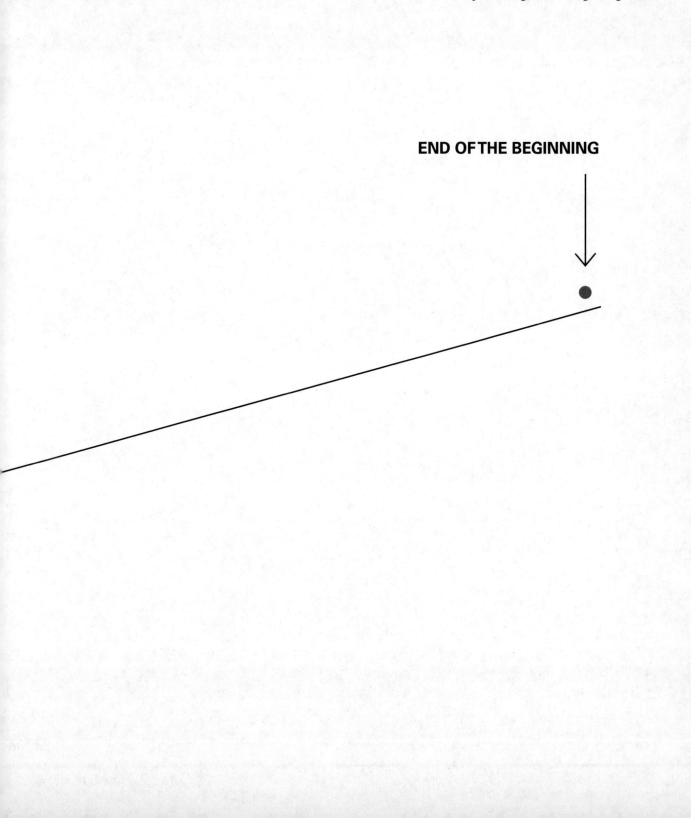

END OF THE BEGINNING

CHAPTER 9
YOU'RE HALFWAY THERE

Plot Whisperer Tweet: *The world is a place in which we learn. Create that place for your readers.*

The Universal Story reflects the eternal structure of life.

As the energy of the story quickens into the middle, the Universal Story demands that the protagonist hope for change. Seduced with promises of something new and different, she is thrust out of where she is at the beginning of the story, both literally and figuratively, into the unknown of the middle.

Details and action in the middle of a story are in stark contrast to the details and action she left in the beginning. She leaves behind all of the expected and scripted perceptions of how to manipulate her experiences. Whether ambivalent or eager about her decision—or lack of one—to move forward, she enters the unknown.

The middle of a story generally spans one-half of a complete story. The middle scenes serve as an archetypal force to accomplish one specific role—induce change.

Plot elements introduced in scenes throughout the beginning of the story deepen and continue in the middle to foreshadow what comes at the end.

The Two Parts of the Middle

The middle of the story is divided into two parts, each with its own energetic marker. The first part is defined by the exotic world of the antagonists. This part is intended to strengthen the protagonist for what is coming. She recommits to reaching her goal; once she does this, the second part of the middle kicks off. This second part of the middle ends with a death. (Note that the death is not always literal.)

Four Plot Tricks for the First Half of the Story

CREATE AN EXOTIC WORLD

In the middle story, the protagonist experiences a mysterious new world through her senses, moment by moment drawing in the sights and tastes and smells and touch of the newness and mystery around her. Until she feels the changes she is experiencing in her heart, which most dramatically happens later, she sees and senses only the surface of things.

The same spark that changes the seasons each year awakens in the protagonist an excitement and trepidation of adventure. As she soars into the middle of the story free of the expected and willing to risk change, she flies into territories of true otherness.

Setting Within the Exotic World

The more completely strange and challenging the setting of the exotic new world, the better. The new world performs the primary function of the middle: to induce change. As such, it is a place of struggle and resistance.

The protagonist's difficulty or ease in maneuvering in the new world says a lot about her struggles ahead. The more she resists the coming change, the greater the degree of tension she will feel as she moves forward into the story.

Whereas the setting in the beginning usually reflects the protagonist, this new setting is controlled by the antagonists. Thus, all the rules, customs, expectations, and punishments of this new setting reflect the antagonist's world. To be successful, the protagonist must master them.

The protagonist's new setting has an immediate effect on her. All its challenges begin molding her into a different form. The rhythm of her mind and the sensitivities of her heart that her old setting induced in her at the beginning of the story serve in stark contrast to the discord now playing in her mind.

CREATE CHALLENGING ANTAGONISTS

The middle story is the territory of the antagonists, which means that the antagonists control the new and unusual world. In this world, antagonists—internal and external—interfere with the protagonist's forward progress, creating tension and excitement. This back-and-forth between protagonist and antagonist forms the essential dynamic yin and yang of stories.

DEVELOP SECONDARY CHARACTERS AND SUBPLOTS

Secondary characters serve as both:

1. Allies
2. Antagonists

Allies support the protagonist's forward movement. Antagonists interfere with her.

The secondary characters also have their own personal goals beyond the function they serve for the protagonist. Allies' goals often reflect those of the protagonist, while antagonists' goals always are in direct opposition to those of the protagonist.

As much as the protagonist's various plot lines control the story, secondary characters' goals also propel the story forward and help define the story's dramatic action plot.

Often secondary characters begin and end their own plot lines in the middle of a story. Subplots in the middle complement and challenge, mirror and deflect those aspects of the protagonist she needs to better understand. The plot line for the major antagonist or villain always continues to the climax.

The secondary characters reflect lessons the protagonist needs to learn and the abilities she can most easily develop. A secondary character often reflects the natural and usually hidden abilities in the protagonist. A secondary character mirrors potentials within the protagonist she has forgotten or lost or was robbed of.

THEME

In Chapter 6 you identified the themes in the beginning portion of your story that reflect the overall thematic meaning of the story. You created symbols, metaphors and similes, and moods that define what your story is about. Readers, as they read, transform these symbols into concepts and ideas that go into the development of your theme. Some themes introduced in the beginning continue into the middle of a story. Others, from the beginning of the story, drop off in the middle.

As much as the themes in the middle deepen and contrast with the themes at the beginning, they also foreshadow what comes at the crisis and also what will happen at the climax at the end.

Your Turn

In this chapter, you'll go through three exercises:

1. Complete the Exotic World Checklist.
2. Continue tracking scenes to and including the recommitment scene.
3. Plot middle scenes on the Plot Planner.

Exotic World Checklist

Do not feel you have to fill in every single question and prompt in the Exotic World Checklist. These are simply considerations that apply to the development of the middle of your story. The questions are intended to spark creativity.

Write the answers that come quickly and clearly for the first half of the middle of your story. As you work on your project, revisit the questions often.

After you're done, switch to the Scene Tracker to track the middle scenes of the story. As you track your scenes, always keep in mind how the plot elements in the middle of your story contrast and foreshadow plot elements that will appear at the end.

Exotic World Checklist

What setting best epitomizes the exotic new world of the middle?

_____

Describe in a couple of sentences the setting of the middle of your story.

_____

How far apart is the old world to the new exotic world in miles?

_____

In mindset?

_____

How does the setting your protagonist enters differ from the setting she just left?

_____

How is the energy of your story different in the new world as compared to the energy in the old world?

_____

What is the atmosphere like in this new setting where the story takes place now?

_____

How have you demonstrated that the change from the old setting to the new setting is irrevocable and permanent?

_____

What sights, sounds, tastes, smells, and textures best epitomize the new world?

_____

What about the new world excites concern and compassion in the protagonist?

_____

And in the reader?

_____

What main action takes place at this setting?

_____

How does the setting in the middle contrast and foreshadow what comes later in the story and at the end?

_____

THEMES

List the themes introduced at the beginning of your story that continue into the middle:

_____

_____

List any new themes that crop up in the middle:

_____

_____

List symbols, metaphors and similes, and authentic details that convey the themes listed.

_____

_____

_____

List any places and objects that best epitomize the overall meaning of your story that appear in the beginning and reappear in the middle.

_____

_____

_____

How do these middle symbols, metaphors and similes, and details contrast and foreshadow what comes at the end?

_____

_____

_____

As you continue to track your scenes on a Scene Tracker, look for ways to switch up details you listed in the last column for the middle scenes to reflect the thematic significance of your story.

_____

_____

_____

_____

PROTAGONIST

How does the protagonist enter the middle of the story? Confused? Fearful? Excited? Sad? Hopeful?

_____

How open is the protagonist to the changes in the setting and themes that now surround her?

_____

Does the protagonist show a passionate engagement or an aversion to the unknown ahead of her now that she is in the middle of the story?

_____

Who is the protagonist now in the middle of the story compared to who the character is at the beginning?

_____

Who is the protagonist now in the middle of the story compared to who she becomes at the end of the story?

_____

What personal fear, flaw, and/or prejudice must she become aware of and overcome for her ultimate success at the end of the story?

_____

Which of the previous trait(s) of the protagonist directly impacts the course of the action in the story?

_____

Is this the same trait(s) that tripped her up in the beginning?

_____

How does this trait(s) intensify its interference in the middle of the story?

_____

What flaws or fears in the middle foreshadow and contribute to her crisis that is coming later in the middle?

_____

Where are your protagonist's thoughts?

_____

Where do those thoughts send the energy of the story?

_____

How does what the protagonist believes about life affect what she wants now in the middle of the story?

_____

What about the protagonist intrigues the reader enough to want to continue reading?

_____

PROTAGONIST'S GOALS

What does the protagonist do in the middle?

_____

Why is she doing it?

_____

How does that contrast with what she did at the beginning?

_____

How does that action contrast to what she does at the end?

_____

What does the protagonist want now that she is in the middle of the story?

_____

Who is the protagonist now in the middle of the story compared to who she will be at the end of the story?

_____

Antagonists

List all of the antagonists who control the exotic world of the middle, in order of importance to the plot:

_____

_____

_____

How do the most important antagonists interfere with the protagonist's forward movement toward her goal?

_____

How do the antagonists reflect and foreshadow in the middle the action coming at the end?

_____

Which antagonist(s) triggers the protagonist's fear, flaw, and/or prejudice? How?

_____

Which of the necessary skills, knowledge, and abilities needed by the protagonist for success at the climax does the antagonist embody?

_____

How are the antagonist's personal traits different from the protagonist's traits?

_____

ANTAGONIST'S GOAL

What does the antagonist(s) do in the middle?

_____

Why is she doing it?

_____

How does that contrast to what the antagonist does at the end and why?

_____

What does the antagonist want?

_____

How do the antagonist's goals directly oppose the protagonist's goals?

_____

How much of the middle of the story does an antagonist's subplot encompass?

_____

Allies

What aspects of the protagonist do the allies reflect in the middle of your story?

_____

What lessons that the protagonist needs to prevail at that climax do the allies teach her?

_____

What abilities do the allies have that mirror those abilities the protagonist can most easily develop and use on her way to achieve success?

_____

How do the allies foreshadow the upcoming story events and action?

_____

What do the allies represent in the middle of the story, in contrast to what they represent at the end?

_____

What natural and hidden abilities in the protagonist does the ally mirror?

_____

What potentials within the protagonist (that she has forgotten or lost or was robbed of) do the allies come to restore?

_____

What traits of the protagonist do the allies trigger in the middle?

_____

How are those traits of the protagonist that were introduced in the beginning reflected in the allies in the middle of your story?

_____

ALLY'S GOAL

What does the ally(s) do in the middle?

_____

Why is she doing it?

_____

How does that contrast to what the ally does at the end and why?

_____

What does the ally want?

_____

How do the ally's goals directly oppose or support the protagonist's goals?

_____

How much of the middle of the story does an ally's subplot encompass?

_____

How do the ally's goals propel the story forward in the middle?

_____

How do the ally's goals define the story's dramatic action plot?

_____

How does what the ally does at the beginning of the middle contrast to what she does at the end? Why?

_____

_____

_____

The Recommitment Scene

The first part of the middle ends when the protagonist recommits or—if she is a reluctant traveler—commits for the first time to the adventure.

By the middle of *Faithful Place* by Tana French, Detective Frank of the Dublin Undercover squad is back in Dalkey at the house his ex-wife's father bought them when they were married and lived together as a family with their daughter. The reader senses that it is a place of warmth and love and could be his again. First, Frank must face his past (backstory wound). In the setting of safety and longing, Frank recommits to solving the mystery of the missing suitcase.

Track Your Scenes

The following exercise continues the creation of the Scene Tracker you started in Chapter 7. With the help of your answers to all the questions on the Exotic World Checklist about the middle plot elements of your project, begin tracking your middle scenes.

Use middle scenes up to and including the second energetic marker. Anchor the last scene on the last line of the last Scene Tracker template with your recommitment scene.

Plot the First Half of the Middle Scenes on the Plot Planner

After you have tracked your scenes for the first half of the middle scenes of your story, next plot your middle scenes up to and including the recommitment scene on the Plot Planner provided. Condense the elements for the middle scenes you generated on the Scene Tracker into one word or phrase. Print the phrase on a mini-sticky note. In order, place each scene above or below the Plot Planner line for the beginning of your story.

If you marked an "X" under the conflict column of the Scene Tracker, place the scene above the line of the Plot Planner.

If there is no "X" in the conflict column of the Scene Tracker, put the scene below the Plot Planner line.

Figure 2. Scene Tracker Template
Copyright © 2004, Martha Alderson

Project Name:

Date:

Draft:

SCENE TRACKER

Chapter:

Scene/ Summary	Dates/Setting	Character Emotional Development	Goal
SCENE 1			
SCENE 2			
SCENE 3			
OPTIONAL			
OPTIONAL			

Notes:

Dramatic/ Action Plot	Conflict	Emotional Change	Thematic Significance/Details

Figure 2. Scene Tracker Template
Copyright © 2004, Martha Alderson

Project Name:

Date:

Draft:

SCENE TRACKER

Chapter:

Scene/ Summary	Dates/Setting	Character Emotional Development	Goal
SCENE 1			
SCENE 2			
SCENE 3			
OPTIONAL			
OPTIONAL			

Notes:

Dramatic/ Action Plot	Conflict	Emotional Change	Thematic Significance/Details

Figure 2. Scene Tracker Template
Copyright © 2004, Martha Alderson

Project Name:

Date:

Draft:

SCENE TRACKER

Chapter:

Scene/ Summary	Dates/Setting	Character Emotional Development	Goal
SCENE 1			
SCENE 2			
SCENE 3			
OPTIONAL			
OPTIONAL			

Notes:

Dramatic/ Action Plot	Conflict	Emotional Change	Thematic Significance/Details

Figure 2. Scene Tracker Template
Copyright © 2004, Martha Alderson

Project Name:

Date:

Draft:

SCENE TRACKER

Chapter:

Scene/ Summary	Dates/Setting	Character Emotional Development	Goal
SCENE 1			
SCENE 2			
SCENE 3			
OPTIONAL			
OPTIONAL			

Notes:

Dramatic/ Action Plot	Conflict	Emotional Change	Thematic Significance/Details

Figure 14. Plot Planner for First Half of the Middle

Working Title: _____

_____

Date: _____

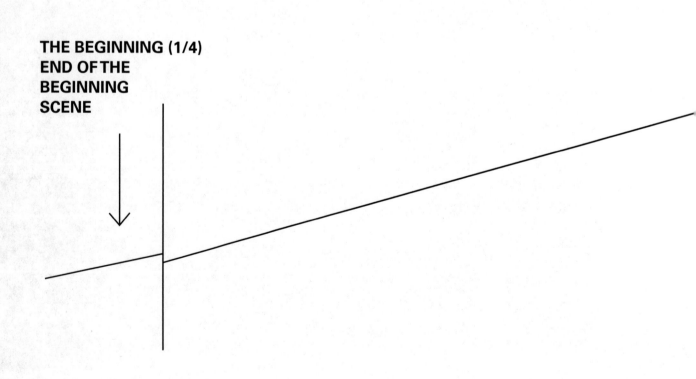

**THE BEGINNING (1/4)
END OF THE
BEGINNING
SCENE**

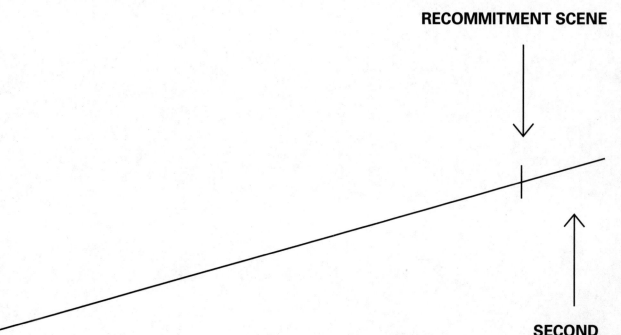

RECOMMITMENT SCENE

**SECOND
HALF OF THE
MIDDLE (1/4)**

FIRST HALF OF THE MIDDLE (1/4)

CHAPTER 10
THE CRISIS IS HERE

Plot Whisperer Tweet: *The protagonist's fears, flaws, and strengths make her believable and represent challenges she must overcome if she's to transform . . . .*

The same Universal Story that calls the light to illuminate the cold, dark night echoes in every protagonist's journey. Your protagonist, too, is destined to shed her old personality and embrace the promise of who she is now.

The first part of the middle defined by the mysterious world of the antagonists continues into the second part of the middle of the story. As we discussed in Chapter 8, the first part is intended to strengthen the protagonist for what is coming. She recommits to reaching her goal; the second part of the middle kicks off. This second part of the middle ends with a death.

Having broken out of the sameness of her previous life and risked the danger of difference, the protagonist recommits to her goal. Now, rather than taking on the same conditioned reflex in which she has always functioned and hoping to rid herself of her pain, she develops a new pattern of behavior and a new way of making decisions.

As she moves steadily toward her goal, a sense of transience—either conscious or merely a whisper—haunts her. Then, suddenly her forward movement is over. The quest she has been on is lost and she with it.

The Universal Story is alive as an eternal echo of all that came before us in the past, all that is now in the present, and all that will be in the future. Think of each of the four parts of a story, represented by the four energetic markers, as reflecting a season of the year. The beginning of the story is like summer. The middle, up to and including the recommitment scene, is fall. The crisis is winter. The climax to come at the end is spring.

As the middle of the Universal Story turns from fall to winter, at around three-quarters of the way through your story, a crisis awaits the protagonist, bleak and severe and edged. Like winter, a crisis is dark within and without, and all appears dead.

Four Plot Tricks

CAULDRON

Often in stories, the crisis is set in the protagonist's hot spot, her cauldron, a place of ultimate transmutation. This hot spot is that one place that holds power over her. In this setting, the protagonist becomes sluggish and slow, and her forward progress sputters to a halt. A hot spot of this magnitude is linked thematically to the protagonist's primary plot and reappears either literally and/or figuratively throughout the story.

In *Faithful Place*, Detective Frank is back at Faithful Place when he suffers his crisis. In that exact place, he comes face-to-face with the truth of his life. The cauldron cracks apart. Frank will never be the same.

ANTAGONISTS' CLIMAX

The ways in which the antagonists interfere with the protagonist's forward progress create subplots that run throughout the middle of the story.

Think of the protagonist's crisis as the antagonist's climax where the antagonist(s) prevails and the protagonist fails. *The protagonist is only as good as the antagonists.*

Throughout the entire beginning and middle of a story, antagonists are always more powerful than the protagonist and seem always to find just the right buttons to push to bring out the worst in the protagonist. After the threshold following the crisis, all that changes. For now . . . the antagonist(s) rule.

The height of the antagonist's power comes at the crisis when the protagonist is confronted by a moment of truth; thereafter, nothing is ever the same.

SHOW OF EMOTION

Writing a crisis scene demands that you get under the protagonist's skin and into her emotions.

At their core, stories are about character transformation. The crisis serves as a slap in the face, a wake-up call to the main character when she becomes aware of life's deeper meaning. Life takes the protagonist by the shoulders and shakes her until she sees life and herself as both really are. The crisis jolts the character into a new acceptance, one in which transformation flourishes. Unless an event creates some sort of learning, awakening, or consciousness, it does not constitute a true crisis.

On your Plot Planner, the energy of your scenes rises in intensity after the second energetic marker at the recommitment scene. During this tumultuous period building up to the crisis, below-the-line scenes of introspection and planning by the protagonist are a thing of the past. Mostly, this is a time when scenes are filled with conflict and tension and high emotion due to obstacles, antagonists, and insights into the character's issues (above-the-line scenes). Each challenge reveals yet more about what the protagonist still needs to learn about herself; or more to the point, needs to relearn and become conscious of in order to prevail at the end of the story.

THE CRISIS

To satisfy the Universal Story, this scene of highest intensity so far in the story generally hits around three-quarters into the entire page count, give or take a breath or two or three, and the energy of the story rises to a breaking point.

The energy in the story coalesces and explodes at the crisis. Sometimes the highest point in the story so far functions primarily on an external dramatic action level. The action at the crisis always reveals more about the protagonist's internal makeup and emotional maturity.

A story is about a character transforming her weaknesses into strengths.

Sometimes the crisis takes the form of two separate events written in two separate scenes. In this case, one scene hits the highest point so far in the story for the dramatic action plot and another scene moves even higher and affects the character's emotional development plot. Possibly the character emotional development crisis comes first and the dramatic action crisis follows. Generally, these two high points occur close together for maximum effect, though sometimes they occur separately and fall further apart.

Your Turn

In this chapter, you're going to perform three exercises:

1. Complete the Crisis Checklist.
2. Track scenes up to and including the crisis.
3. Plot the rest of middle scenes on the Plot Planner.

The Crisis Checklist

Today's date: _____

Working title: _____

CAULDRON

In what setting in the exotic world does the crisis hit?

_____

Describe the crisis setting.

_____

Does that setting represent change for the protagonist?

_____

Does that setting hold any fear for the protagonist?

_____

How does the crisis setting link thematically to the protagonist's primary plot?

_____

Does this same setting appear, either literally and/or figuratively, earlier in the story?

_____

ANTAGONIST'S CLIMAX (AND PROTAGONIST CRISIS)

In one sentence, describe the antagonists' climax.

_____

What part does the antagonist(s) play in the ultimate breakdown of the protagonist?

_____

Does any other antagonist hold even greater power over the protagonist than the one at work at the crisis?

_____

If so, can that antagonist be integrated into the crisis?

_____

SHOW OF EMOTION

How does the energy that coalesces and explodes at the crisis match the emotions the scene creates in the protagonist?

_____

What does the action in the crisis reveal about the character's internal makeup and emotional maturity?

_____

Scan each scene in your story in order from the beginning to the crisis and consider only the part(s) your protagonist plays in her own demise.

What parts of herself does she need to reclaim in order to be whole?

_____

THE CRISIS

How much does the energy of your scenes rise in intensity on your Plot Planner after the second energetic marker of the recommitment scene?

_____

_____

_____

During this tumultuous period building up to the crisis, how many below-the-line scenes of introspection and planning by the protagonist occur?

_____

_____

_____

What happens to the protagonist at the crisis?

_____

_____

_____

List all the reversals in fortune that the protagonist experiences at the crisis.

_____

_____

_____

What beliefs or behaviors are stripped from, lost, or killed in the protagonist due to what happens at the crisis?

_____

_____

_____

Track Scenes Up to and Including the Crisis

Based on the Crisis Checklist and the list of scenes you created in Chapter 3, continue tracking the seven essential plot elements in your middle scenes from the recommitment scene up to and including the crisis scene on the provided Scene Tracker templates. Create and analyze scenes and ideas that make up the last half of the middle of the story.

Use scenes from the recommitment scenes up to and including the third energetic marker. Anchor the last scene on the last line of the last Scene Tracker template with the scenes that follow the crisis and take place before she enters the end and the final push to the climax.

Plot the Remainder of the Middle Scenes on the Plot Planner

First, refer to the picture of the character emotional development transformation on the Plot Planner you created at the end of Chapter 1. Study and, if need be, revise the four pivotal scenes framing your story on the Plot Planner at the end of Chapter 4.

Condense the plot elements for the middle scenes you generated on the Scene Tracker earlier in this chapter into one word or phrase. Print the phrase on a mini-sticky note. In order, plot all the scenes anticipated or found in the middle of your story above and below the line of the Plot Planner and including the crisis.

If you marked an "X" under the conflict column of the Scene Tracker, place the scene above the line of the Plot Planner.

If there is no "X" in the conflict column of the Scene Tracker, put the scene below the Plot Planner line.

<table>
<tr><td>Figure 2. Scene Tracker Template
Copyright © 2004, Martha Alderson</td><td>**Project Name:**
Date:
Draft:</td></tr>
</table>

SCENE TRACKER

Chapter:

Scene/ Summary	Dates/Setting	Character Emotional Development	Goal
SCENE 1			
SCENE 2			
SCENE 3			
OPTIONAL			
OPTIONAL			

Notes:

Dramatic/ Action Plot	Conflict	Emotional Change	Thematic Significance/Details

Figure 2. Scene Tracker Template
Copyright © 2004, Martha Alderson

Project Name:

Date:

Draft:

SCENE TRACKER

Chapter:

Scene/ Summary	Dates/Setting	Character Emotional Development	Goal
SCENE 1			
SCENE 2			
SCENE 3			
OPTIONAL			
OPTIONAL			

Notes:

Dramatic/ Action Plot	Conflict	Emotional Change	Thematic Significance/Details

Figure 2. Scene Tracker Template
Copyright © 2004, Martha Alderson

Project Name:

Date:

Draft:

SCENE TRACKER

Chapter:

Scene/ Summary	Dates/Setting	Character Emotional Development	Goal
SCENE 1			
SCENE 2			
SCENE 3			
OPTIONAL			
OPTIONAL			

Notes:

Dramatic/ Action Plot	Conflict	Emotional Change	Thematic Significance/Details

Figure 2. Scene Tracker Template	Project Name:
Copyright © 2004, Martha Alderson	Date:
	Draft:

SCENE TRACKER

Chapter:

Scene/ Summary	Dates/Setting	Character Emotional Development	Goal
SCENE 1			
SCENE 2			
SCENE 3			
OPTIONAL			
OPTIONAL			

Notes:

Dramatic/ Action Plot	Conflict	Emotional Change	Thematic Significance/Details

Figure 15. Plot Planner for Second Half of the Middle

Working Title: _____

_____

Date: _____

FIRST HALF OF THE MIDDLE (1/4)
RECOMMITMENT SCENE

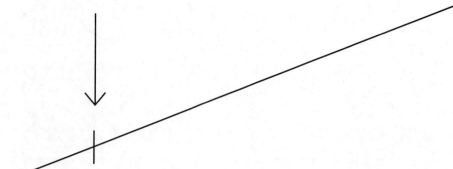

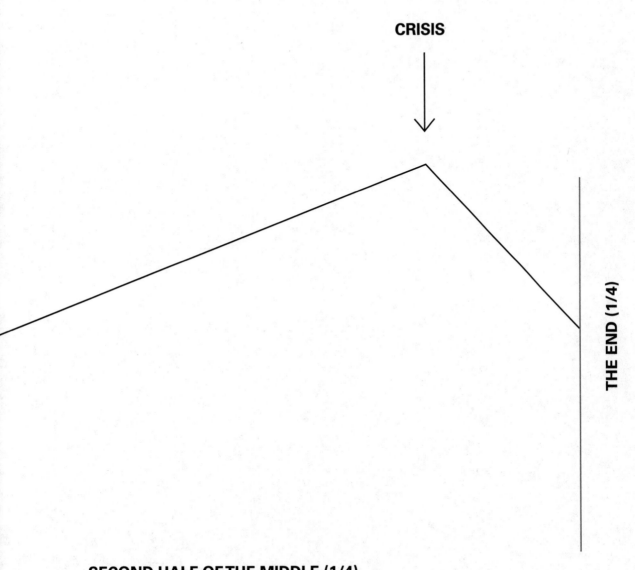

CHAPTER 11

WHAT ARE THE SUBPLOTS?

Plot Whisperer Tweet: *Never repeat. Deepen.*

Subplots do more than simply serve as color. Subplots reflect a different angle of the main thematic significance plot of your story.

Some writers start out knowing exactly who and what they are writing about and stay true to that vision from the beginning to the end. Others write about one character doing one thing, then switch to another character doing something else, and then switch back to the first character or switch to an entirely new person with different action. Switching viewpoints reveals a multitude of sides to a story. Switching too many times leads to a tangled mess.

A major decision required of every writer is to identify the primary plot of her story.

- Through the character
- Through the action
- Through theme
- Through cause and effect
- Through plotting and writing and re-plotting and rewriting and writing some more
- Through meditation

Identifying the primary plot of your story is only part of your work. You also must commit to that plot as being primary. Making this sort of commitment too early may cut off that serendipitous wonder that comes during the generative stage. However, eventually, knowing what your story is about and the ability to articulate that succinctly allows you to focus and unravel knots.

In other words, you know what parts of your story to highlight as the main plot and what to push to the background as a subplot.

Some subplots originate from the protagonist. Subplots also originate from other characters. Subplots proliferate in the middle of the story. The progression of the protagonist's internal flaw or character emotional development plot often serves as a subplot to a dramatic action-driven story in which the primary plot revolves around external action. The dramatic action demands a goal. The character emotional development demands growth.

The protagonist's internal conflict or fatal flaw reveals what she needs to achieve internally in order to reach the goal of the primary plot. The resolution of the primary plot is dependent upon the resolution of the internal subplot.

At the end of the beginning scene, the protagonist believes she has broken away from all the pre-established roles imposed by society at large and is on her way to success. Suddenly, she finds herself surrounded by allies and antagonists who are living other pre-decided roles to varying degrees of success. These secondary characters create subplots that challenge the protagonist's primary plot.

As the protagonist struggles forward toward her goal, she sees in others those traits she is only now learning reside inside of her. For example, a secondary character feels sorry for herself. The protagonist suddenly understands that life isn't treating the secondary character unfairly, just as life isn't treating her unfairly either. In seeing the victim in others, she begins to recognize it in herself.

Secondary Characters

Often subplots in the middle are determined by secondary characters in pursuit of their own goals, which can be in direct opposition to what the protagonist wants. Secondary characters with their own subplots serve to reinforce the thematic significance of the overall story. Secondary characters reflect different aspects of the protagonist.

The protagonist attracts characters who mirror qualities or beliefs she has about life. The things she doesn't like about her fellow characters are reflections of what she does or does not do and what she believes.

A subplot that begins and ends in the middle of the larger story contains a beginning (as the character leaves her ordinary world and enters the exotic world) that leads to a middle. A rise in intensity often corresponds with the second energetic marker of the overall story's primary plot when the protagonist recommits to the journey. A subplot that lasts only as long as the middle culminates energetically just before the third energetic marker of the primary plot's crisis. (Do not confuse a crisis with the climax. The climax comes at the end of the overall story itself and shows the character fully confident in her own personal power. The crisis shows the protagonist at her worst—after all, it *is* a crisis.)

SECONDARY CHARACTERS SUPPORT THE PROTAGONIST'S EMOTIONAL DEVELOPMENT

Secondary characters' subplots create depth in a piece of writing when they tie into and support the development of the primary character (better understood as the protagonist's character emotional development).

For example: A writer develops a secondary character based on patients he worked with in a previous day job. He has terrific authentic details, having spent so much time with one particular patient with special needs. The character (who is the protagonist's sister) is of great emotional importance to the protagonist. (The writer is doing what has long been espoused as a good practice for writers—write what you know.)

The writer's front story (dramatic action plot) centers around drugs, money laundering and shady operations, guns and prison, and betrayal. He demonstrates writing strength in developing dramatic action. When asked who his audience is, the writer has not yet considered the matter. The front story is high-stakes exciting intrigue, which often resonates with male readers. Yet the protagonist is a woman. She is a "ballsy" woman to be sure, confident and fearless.

When asked how much of his story he wants to involve in the other two plot lines—character emotional development (which, at this point, is little, if at all, developed) and thematic significance—he has no answers. He has the same reaction in response to questions about whether he plans to include a romantic secondary plot line in his story.

The writer, in our example, tries to solve the problem by introducing and developing a secondary character: a special-needs sister of the protagonist. This helps bring heart to the protagonist's character and thus, develop her character emotional development plot. But because he writes what he knows about patients with special needs, the writer concentrates on describing the sister's behavior almost in isolation and without tying those elements to the protagonist or giving the reader a sense of impact those behaviors have on the protagonist. Even more important is the effect the sister's special needs had on the protagonist's backstory development.

Because the sister does not play directly into the dramatic action plot (in other words, her afflictions are not necessary for the development of the primary plot), rather than devote so much time to the development of the secondary character, he would be better off using the sister's afflictions to deepen the reader's understanding and appreciation of the protagonist. Her backstory wound, being ignored by her parents in favor of attending to the sister's special needs, bleeds into her everyday life.

Subplots, whether the protagonist's or of a secondary character, must complement the protagonist's primary plot.

Ultimately, the protagonist of a story is required to rid from her life her self-limiting patterns and habits and beliefs. As the protagonist changes, many of these secondary characters leave her life, making room in the story for the primary plot to shine. Thus, subplots often begin and end in the middle of the story. The protagonist leaves the middle of the story for the end, banged up but also strengthened and provided with all she needs. Now she eliminates anyone and anything in the way of her final goal.

One subplot reflects a secondary character going after her goal while having something the protagonist wants. Another subplot shows a character expressing anger and resentment when thwarted from achieving what she wants. These two subplots mirror the protagonist's push toward change and transformation.

Some writers make the mistake of writing too thin—writing about only the steps a character takes without using subplots. Other writers drown the story with too many plots and subplots.

If your story primarily is about the protagonist's external goal of solving a mystery, the mystery is the primary plot and the focus of the story. Too much delving into the protagonist's past or focusing on flaws overshadows the mystery and slows it down. This means that the protagonist's internal plot and romance plot stay in the background.

Often in stories, the protagonist starts out wanting one thing and then, because of what she encounters in the story, switches goals. The first goal, now a subplot of its own, comes to fruition around the time of the protagonist's great awakening—character emotional development crisis.

After the pain of the crisis, and just as the pieces of the mystery or the main dilemma or her life begin to make sense to her and the light of consciousness snaps on, her original goal is met and the protagonist wins the material gain toward which she first had worked. She accepts the elevated level of personal power or the award or prize or admiration or any other sort of physical or psychological gratification.

Now, however, because of her awakening, the things she once coveted do not fulfill her as she once thought they would. The answer she sought is no longer important. The man she longed for no longer appeals to her. She sees others lost in the roles they play. That which she dreamed would bring her fulfillment doesn't. Thus, what she expected to feel like a crowning achievement leaves her cold, perhaps even feeling frustrated and angry, slapped with an inner sensation of lack and emptiness.

In finding what she does not want, thanks to the story's subplots, the protagonist refines what she *does* want in the main plot. This then drives the story to completion in the final quarter of the story.

CREATE SUBPLOT WEBS

The more aware you are of the subplots, who they belong to, and what they represent in the story, the better able you are to use the subplots to create cohesion, tension and meaning.

The oval in the middle of the sample subplot web states the primary plot and indicates whether a story is primarily about solving a murder, getting the guy, landing the job, flying into space, getting over a death, learning acceptance, extending forgiveness, or life.

Notice that the sample subplot web is divided in half; the upper half reflects all the different antagonists' subplots and the lower half reflects all the different allies' subplots. Where one subplot creates another subplot, a line is drawn to link the two subplots together. Each one of these subplots reveals yet a different side of the protagonist and offers a full range of his world to create depth and thematic meaning to the overall story.

Your Turn

Fill in the subplot web for the allies and the antagonists of your story. These allies and antagonists can be other characters. Their subplots can be any positive or negative plot elements you are interested in developing into a subplot that will bring depth and meaning to the primary plot.

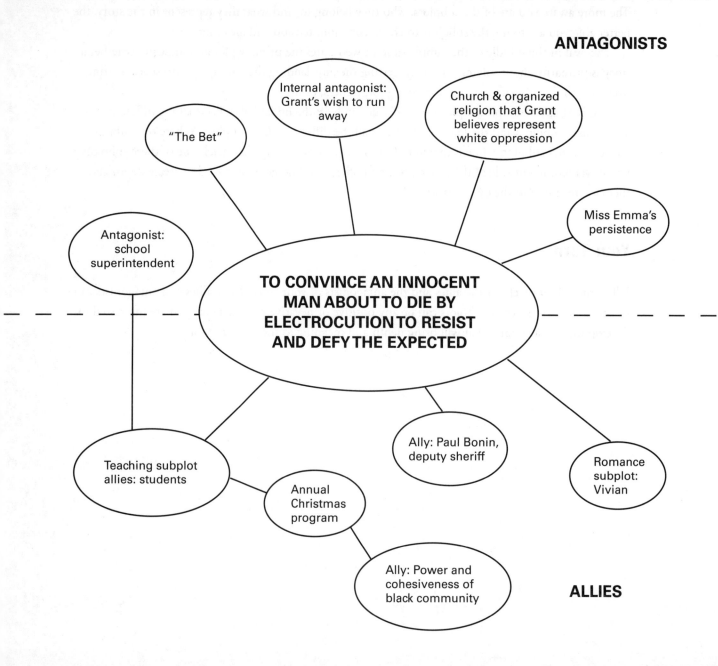

Figure 16. Subplots Web
A Lesson Before Dying by Ernest J. Gaines

ANTAGONISTS

"The Bet"

Internal antagonist: Grant's wish to run away

Church & organized religion that Grant believes represent white oppression

Miss Emma's persistence

Antagonist: school superintendent

TO CONVINCE AN INNOCENT MAN ABOUT TO DIE BY ELECTROCUTION TO RESIST AND DEFY THE EXPECTED

Teaching subplot allies: students

Annual Christmas program

Ally: Paul Bonin, deputy sheriff

Romance subplot: Vivian

Ally: Power and cohesiveness of black community

ALLIES

Figure 17. Subplots Web

Working Title: _____

Date: _____

ANTAGONISTS

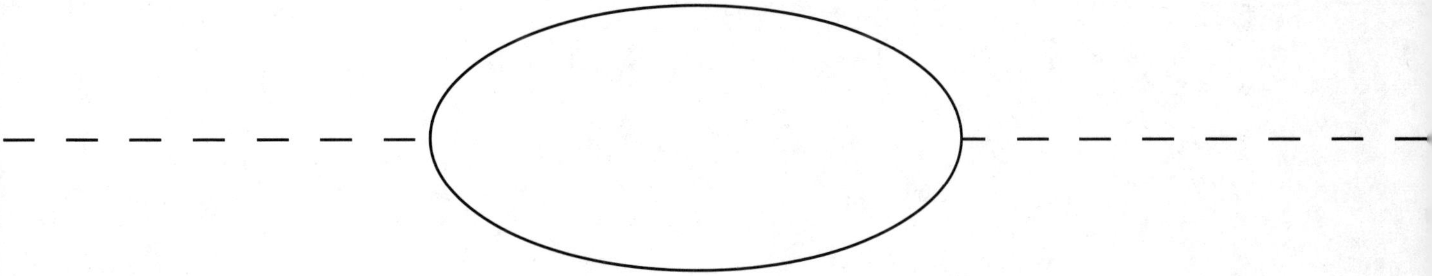

ALLIES

Working Title

Date

ANTAGONISTS

ALLIES

CHAPTER 12

WE'RE AT THE END

Plot Whisperer Tweet: *You don't know what you're writing until you reach the end.*

The Universal Story moves in a rhythm set by nature. Beginnings flow like lost echoes of summer wandering into the agitation of fall and the middle. From the bleak winter of the crisis, the protagonist's true self emerges in a slow beat as she inches her way toward the first warmth of spring.

The protagonist enters the final quarter of the story in search of a way of living and being that best expresses her newfound vitality and promise. Now, after surviving the crisis, she is without the need of any mask, of pretense or falsities. Now that the ultimate transformation has begun in earnest, her true character emerges and the story deepens with a clear and refined vision of the end.

The journey has been dangerous and slow. Having seen an inkling of her true self, a new identity begins to form. Possibilities emerge that bring her nearer to her destination. The challenge for her now is to find the answers and seize the prize. The protagonist welcomes the full challenge of the final frontier with patience and inspiration. Worthy of her energy and heart, the trials ahead of her at the end refine her transformation with tests and wonder.

The end of a story serves as an archetypal force to accomplish one specific role—transformation.

Path to the Climax

Now that she has survived the crisis, the protagonist trusts herself and discerns traces of a way out of the darkness and into the light. In her instincts about the shape of the final challenges that await her, she creates a new path forward. She crosses the threshold and enters the end of the story, the first of many steps still to be taken before reaching the climax and resolution at the end.

One of the defining elements of the final quarter of a story is that the protagonist is slapped with a number of complications the nearer she moves toward achieving her goal. With each complication, the protagonist suffers some sort of reversal. At each reversal in the middle of the story, the protagonist loses power and is physically, mentally, or emotionally restrained or injured.

However, now in the final quarter of the story, though she may be knocked off track and suffering, the protagonist spots gifts and opportunities open to her that she refused before, forgot, or never recognized. From the power she accumulates from her interactions with allies and positive forces throughout the entire book—and especially at the end—she no longer fights against the opposition. In the buildup to the climax, the protagonist finds ways to overcome her antagonists without force.

When she enters the final quarter of the story, she has assessed her past plans and goals for the purpose of creating a right and appropriate future. To succeed she must face her greatest fear in order never to fear again. As the protagonist moves toward the climax, she is focused and filled with purpose. She knows what she needs to do and she knows she is the only one who can do it. In doing what is needed at the climax, she fulfills her unique destiny.

This clarity and single-minded focus does not belie the truth of the travail and turbulence she meets along the way. Great risk is required as is great suffering before she reaches the climax.

What started at the beginning of the story when the protagonist first set out seems so simple and clear now. In the middle of the story, she often turned ambivalent as the new world's complexity and challenges unfolded. Still, she never stopped moving nearer and nearer to her crowning glory. In changing the choices she made and sacrificing the familiar, she transformed her life. She knew what she was doing. Now her passion is clear and creative.

The climax is what all the other scenes in the story add up to in the end.

Unexpected Ending

A climax is best when it is completely unexpected and at the same time entirely expected. Foreshadowing throughout the story prepares the reader for what comes at the climax. The protagonist has given herself to the completion of her goal. She is absorbed in her experience of moving forward, putting one foot in front of another. Scene by scene, through cause and effect, each new step is foreshadowed, strengthening its grip on finality. Finally, the climax hits. The protagonist may feel ambushed but never the reader.

When the protagonist and her greatest foe meet, the forces present at the climax are at their greatest for both the protagonist and the antagonist. The more opposing the forces or the greater the magnitude of the forces in opposition, the more exciting the climax is for the reader and the audience. The character with the greatest self-knowledge triumphs. The level of this triumph is equal to the level of opposing forces. If the opposing forces are a near match for the protagonist, the triumph will be modest. The more powerful the opposing forces, the greater the triumph.

At the climax, every conviction and instinct the protagonist has is tested. The climax shows the protagonist in action that reflects her transformed self. Throughout the story, the protagonist's flaw and beliefs limit her and she lives diminished by her backstory wound; yet throughout she is building wholeness. The climax shows her finally healed.

Such endings offer great promise and a new beginning the reader never could have anticipated, and a new story begins. In this way, although the story seems at an end, none of it will ever be lost. The protagonist and her story continue beyond the endings on the page.

Resolution

A few forces do not converge at the climax, but instead gather afterward during the falling energy at the end of the book. This last scene(s) makes up the final downward line on the Plot Planner after the climax.

For the reader to feel satisfied at the end of a story, she must be able to assess how the story world looks and acts now that the protagonist is not who she was at the start of things. The denouement gives value and a point to the finished piece. The reader wants to know where the energy is going now that the protagonist has gained self-knowledge and how much strength she has now that she has been transformed. If the protagonist was triumphant at the climax, any lesser characters who had a positive effect on the protagonist also meet with success.

In *Faithful Place*, Detective Frank ends the story by closing the door to Number 16 one last time, a symbolic gesture, acknowledging the healing of his backstory wound.

Your Turn

At this point, you'll perform three exercises:

1. Complete the exit checklist.
2. Finish tracking scenes, up to and including the resolution scene.
3. Finish your story's Plot Planner.

Fill in the following exit checklist for the end of your story.

Exit Checklist

SETTING

Describe in a couple of sentences the setting at the end of your story.

_____

_____

What does the setting represent to the protagonist?

_____

_____

What does the setting at the end of the book represent and convey about her choices and afflictions and circumstances?

_____

_____

What main action takes place at this setting at the end?

_____

_____

What mood does this setting instill in the reader?

_____

_____

Is the climax set somewhere that symbolizes the protagonist's cauldron?

_____

_____

_____

Where does the resolution take place?

_____

_____

_____

THEMES

List the themes of the final one-quarter of your story.

_____

_____

_____

_____

List those themes that run from the beginning to the end of your story.

_____

_____

_____

List any themes that appear at the end that you now plan to incorporate into the beginning.

_____

_____

_____

List the symbols, metaphors, and similes used to convey the themes just listed.

_____

_____

_____

_____

PROTAGONIST

Name:

_____

How does the protagonist enter the final quarter of the story? With trepidation? Confidence?

_____

Which transformed trait(s) of the character directly impacts the climax of the story?

_____

What skills, knowledge, and abilities does she need for success at the climax?

_____

What does the character do in the scenes that lead up to the climax?

_____

What makes her believe the steps she takes will get her to where she wants to be?

_____

What does the character do at the climax?

_____

Why is she doing it?

_____

What does the character do after the climax that shows what the story world looks like now that she has transformed?

_____

Do her goals propel the story to the ending?

_____

How do her goals define the story's dramatic action plot?

_____

What is the greatest self-knowledge she gains as she triumphs at the climax?

_____

SECONDARY CHARACTERS

List the major secondary characters who appear in the final quarter of the story.

_____

_____

_____

_____

_____

What aspects of the protagonist do the secondary characters reflect at the end of your story?

_____

_____

_____

What lessons do the secondary characters have that reflect what the protagonist has learned and uses to prevail at that climax?

_____

_____

_____

Did any secondary character mirror the natural and often hidden abilities in the protagonist or serve to remind the protagonist about the potential within her that was forgotten or lost or taken away?

_____

_____

_____

CLIMAX

List the complications that occur in the final quarter of the story as the protagonist nears the climax and achieves her goal.

_____

_____

_____

Who/what is the protagonist's greatest foe?

_____

Does she meet that foe at the climax?

_____

How great are the opposing forces at the climax?

_____

How great is the magnitude of the forces in opposition?

_____

_____

Does this build excitement at the climax?

_____

_____

_____

RESOLUTION

Who is the protagonist after the climax settles in the final pages of the story?

_____

_____

_____

Track Scenes Up to and Including the Resolution

Based on the Exit Checklist you just filled in and the list of scenes you created in Chapter 3, finish tracking the seven essential plot elements in all the story scenes on the provided Scene Tracker templates. Create and analyze scenes and ideas that make up end of the story.

Use scenes from the beginning of the end, including the fourth energetic marker. Anchor the last scene on the last line of the last Scene Tracker template with the scene that resolves the story.

Finish Your Story's Plot Planner

Now that you have tracked all your scenes, refer to the picture you created at the end of Chapter 1 of the character emotional development transformation on the Plot Planner. Study the sequence of change in the protagonist. If need be, revise the four pivotal scenes framing your story on the Plot Planner at the end of Chapter 4.

1. Condense the plot elements on the Scene Tracker for the ending scenes into one word or phrase. Print the phrase on a mini-sticky note. In order, place each scene above or below the Plot Planner line for the end of your story.
2. Plot all the ending scenes, including the climax and resolution scenes above and below the line of the Plot Planner.

If you marked an "X" under the conflict column of the Scene Tracker, place the scene above the line of the Plot Planner.

If there is no "X" in the conflict column of the Scene Tracker, put the scene below the Plot Planner line.

<table>
<tr><td>**Figure 2. Scene Tracker Template**
Copyright © 2004, Martha Alderson</td><td>**Project Name:**</td></tr>
<tr><td></td><td>**Date:**</td></tr>
<tr><td></td><td>**Draft:**</td></tr>
</table>

SCENE TRACKER

Chapter:

Scene/ Summary	Dates/Setting	Character Emotional Development	Goal
SCENE 1			
SCENE 2			
SCENE 3			
OPTIONAL			
OPTIONAL			

Notes:

Dramatic/ Action Plot	Conflict	Emotional Change	Thematic Significance/Details

Figure 2. Scene Tracker Template
Copyright © 2004, Martha Alderson

Project Name:

Date:

Draft:

SCENE TRACKER

Chapter:

Scene/ Summary	Dates/Setting	Character Emotional Development	Goal
SCENE 1			
SCENE 2			
SCENE 3			
OPTIONAL			
OPTIONAL			

Notes:

Dramatic/ Action Plot	Conflict	Emotional Change	Thematic Significance/Details

Figure 2. Scene Tracker Template
Copyright © 2004, Martha Alderson

Project Name:

Date:

Draft:

SCENE TRACKER

Chapter:

Scene/ Summary	Dates/Setting	Character Emotional Development	Goal
SCENE 1			
SCENE 2			
SCENE 3			
OPTIONAL			
OPTIONAL			

Notes:

Dramatic/ Action Plot	Conflict	Emotional Change	Thematic Significance/Details

Figure 2. Scene Tracker Template
Copyright © 2004, Martha Alderson

Project Name:

Date:

Draft:

SCENE TRACKER

Chapter:

Scene/ Summary	Dates/Setting	Character Emotional Development	Goal
SCENE 1			
SCENE 2			
SCENE 3			
OPTIONAL			
OPTIONAL			

Notes:

Dramatic/ Action Plot	Conflict	Emotional Change	Thematic Significance/Details

Figure 18. Plot Planner for the End

Working Title: _____

Date: _____

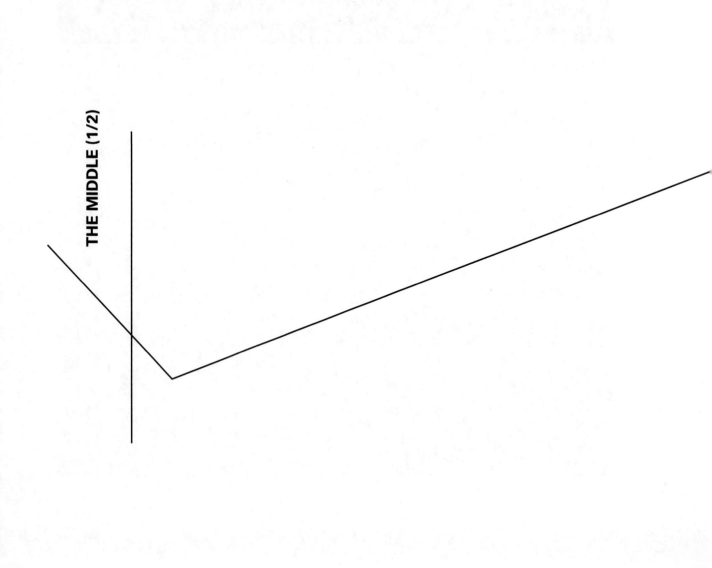

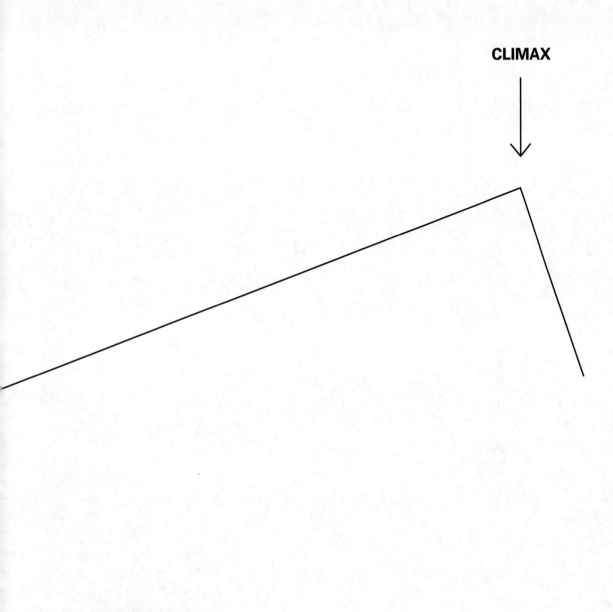

CLIMAX

THE END (1/4)

PART III

Analyzing Your Plot

CHAPTER 13

IT'S ABOUT CAUSE AND EFFECT

Plot Whisperer Tweet: *Link scenes by cause and effect & each scene becomes organic = from the seeds you plant in the first scene grow the fruit of the next scene.*

You have created checklists and ticked off the plot elements for each part of your story. All the scenes of your story have been tracked on Scene Trackers and then arranged in a linear pattern on Plot Planners. Now, if you haven't already begun, you're ready to write your story. At the same time, continue working to the end of this workbook.

Throughout Part III, you'll evaluate the entire project based on all the individual plot pieces. You'll test the cause and effect of your story, the theme, the climax, and the protagonist's backstory for a deeper understanding of the different layers of your story. In this chapter, we deal primarily with cause and effect.

The Universal Story is satisfying because it gives story events a structure and suggests causes for them. For every action, there is an opposite and equal reaction; for every cause, an effect. A story is made up of a series of scenes moving the characters forward in moment-to-moment action. Rather than each scene vanishing as the next scene replaces it and the story unraveling, your scenes must be connected together so that each builds on the other. Ensure each plot element follows logically from one to the other.

The following exercises will help you analyze your story and scenes from four different cause and effect angles. This will give you an advantage when determining which scenes best link to others by cause and effect, which scenes link in an apparently more haphazard sequencing, and which scenes need no linkage at all.

Three Types of Stories

When analyzing the cause and effect of a story, it is best to keep in mind the type of story you are writing: action-driven, character-driven, or a balance of the two.

In an action-driven story, external action through physical movement causes other external actions to happen. For the most part, the protagonist is left emotionally unchanged at the end. (Think of the James Bond stories as the epitome of this kind of story.)

In a character-driven story, emotional reactive expression causes the protagonist's ultimate change and transformation at the end.

In a balanced story, external action interacts with the protagonist, and the protagonist's reactions affect the external action. All of this ultimately changes and transforms her at the end.

Analyze the Energy of a Story

As you complete the exercises in this workbook, you'll find yourself cutting and adding story ideas. It is not uncommon for the scene arrangement of a story to shift back and forth, even in the third and fourth drafts. Remain flexible as you imagine your story and develop the plot and structure. Be adaptive as you re-imagine your story from the character's point of view and from the action and theme. As you settle on the overall form and function of your scenes and story, each change you make affects the placement of the four energetic markers. Always keep in mind the flow of energy in the Universal Story and how all the parts of your story play into the whole.

The first energetic marker and the end of the beginning scene leads to the second energetic marker, the recommitment scene. The recommitment scene leads to the third energetic marker, the crisis, and the crisis leads to the fourth energetic marker, the climax.

SCENES PRECEDING AND FOLLOWING ENERGETIC MARKERS

One scene prepares for another and sets up anticipation in the reader of something to come. A follow-up scene shows the full impact of the event on the character—both physically and emotionally. Preparation and anticipation generate tension, conflict, and suspense.

Keep this sequence in mind as you analyze the cause and effect surrounding each energetic marker:

- Preparation and anticipation
- Energetic marker and main event
- Reaction and follow-through

CAUSE AND EFFECT SCENE BY SCENE

Cause and effect within and between scenes allows you to seamlessly lead the reader to each major turning point by linking the cause in one scene to the effect in the next scene. This sequencing allows the energy of the story to rise smoothly. If the sequence breaks down, scenes come out of the blue, and your story turns episodic. The reader, in turn, becomes disconcerted.

A story is made up of scenes with a clear dependence on each other. Conflict in a scene represents the motivating cause that sets a series of events in motion.

As you test for cause and effect notice how some features of your story are more important than others. Look for patterns and see what elements lead to the thematic significance and which do not.

SCENES WITH NO CAUSE AND EFFECT

As important as it is to study how scenes are linked by cause and effect, it's just as important to analyze scenes with no line(s) linking them to others. Note any unexpected objects, locations, and actions in and between scenes deserve foreshadowing and earlier mentions and hints.

The reader (and the protagonist) doesn't have an outline of the story and thus can only anticipate what is coming by discerning the clues given along the way by the use of foreshadowing. The life of the story takes on its own particular shape, and its sequence seems inevitable to the reader and audience because of foreshadowing.

EMOTIONAL CAUSE AND EFFECT

Use cause and effect to convey emotion in the protagonist. In one scene, a character responds emotionally to an event. In the next scene, we see the outcome of that emotional response, which, in turn, becomes the cause for another emotional effect. Each scene is organic; seeds planted in the first scene create the effect in the next.

Your Turn

Once again, push aside the words of your story. This time, stand back from it to determine the causality between scenes and the overall coherence of your story. View your story as a whole. With such an insight, you are better able to turn scenes with emotionally rich characters who are experiencing conflict into the driving force behind an exceptional story.

ANALYZE THE CAUSE AND EFFECT OF YOUR STORY

Check the type of story you are writing and explain why:

☐ Action-driven?

_____

_____

☐ Character-driven?

_____

_____

☐ Balanced combination of the two?

_____

_____

Your answer to what type of story you are writing helps determine the different demands and considerations regarding the cause and effect of your story.

- In a purely action-driven story, consider cause and effect through the dramatic action level for the external events and their consequences.

- In a character-driven story, take into account how the protagonist's character emotional development causes and affects her emotional state.
- For balance, keep the entire scope of your story in your mind as you analyze the cause and effect between the characters and the action of your story.

ENERGETIC MARKERS

Refer to Chapter 4 for your revised scene placements for the four energetic markers. Re-evaluate that placement yet again. This time, change and/or adapt any scenes necessary to reflect the significance of these four major turning points in relationship to each other, both from looking forward and from looking backward, too.

Place the changes you made in the four energetic markers in their proper sequence based on logical cause and effect on the Plot Planner that follows.

Answer the following questions about the cause and effect of your energetic markers:

1. How does the end of the beginning scene at the first energetic marker lead to the recommitment scene at the second energetic marker?

_____

_____

_____

2. How does the recommitment scene at the second energetic marker lead to the third energetic marker, the crisis?

_____

_____

_____

3. How does the crisis at the third energetic marker lead to the climax at the fourth energetic marker?

_____

_____

_____

Figure 9. Plot Planner—Energetic Markers

Working Title: _____

_____

Date: _____

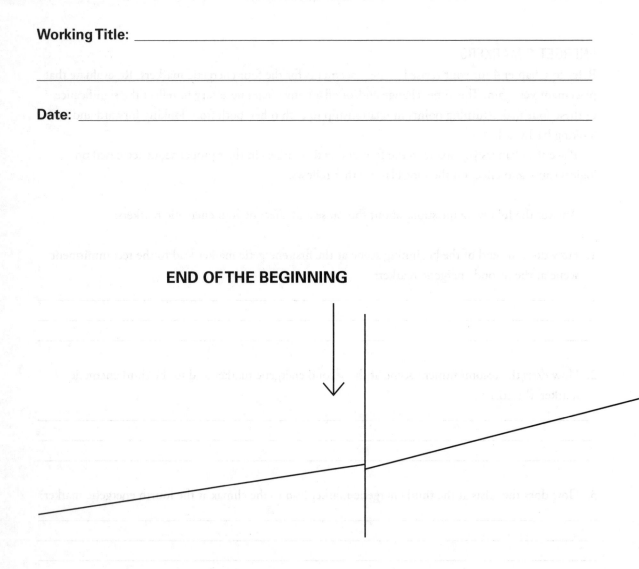

END OF THE BEGINNING

THE BEGINNING (1/4)

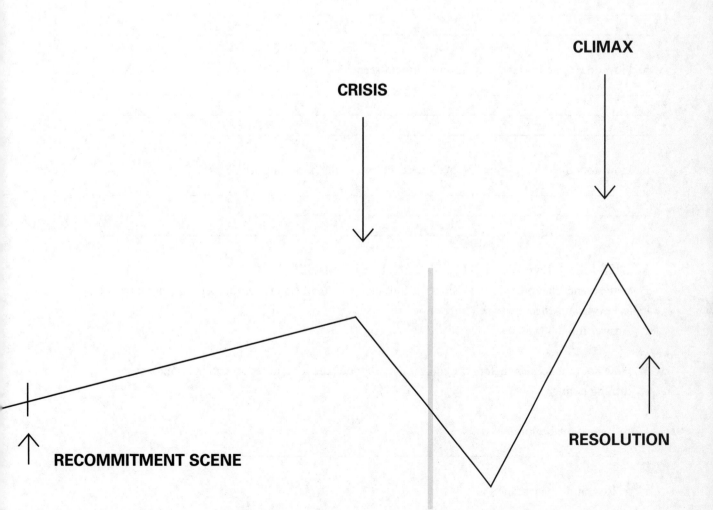

4. How does the climax at the end reflect the crisis?

_____

_____

_____

5. How does the crisis reflect the recommitment scene?

_____

_____

_____

6. How does the recommitment scene reflect the end of the beginning scene?

_____

_____

_____

SCENES PRECEDING AND FOLLOWING ENERGETIC MARKERS

Place the scenes that precede and follow the four energetic markers in their proper sequence based on logical cause and effect on your Plot Planner.

Answer the following:

1. How does the scene(s) before the energetic marker prepare for and set up anticipation of the turning point?

- End of the beginning

_____

- Recommitment scene

_____

- Crisis

_____

- Climax

_____

2. How does the follow-up scene(s) after each energetic marker show the full impact of the event on the character both:

- Physically

- Emotionally

CAUSE AND EFFECT, SCENE BY SCENE

Place the rest of the scenes in your story in their proper sequence based on logical cause and effect for the beginning, middle, and end of your story.

Feel free to refer to the previous Plot Planners you've developed. Test the cause and effect of the scenes in each part and deepen your understanding of the cause and effect layer of your story.

Each time one scene causes another scene, draw a line on the Plot Planner connecting the two scenes together. Observe the lacework of scenes. Determine which scenes:

- Directly link to others by cause and effect
- Link together in a more haphazard sequencing of cause and effect
- Need no linkage at all

SCENES WITH NO CAUSE AND EFFECT

Stand back from your Plot Planner and analyze the scenes. Where there is a break in the pacing back and forth between scenes, certain scenes link indirectly and often from far apart. Foreshadowing creates jumps between the cause—showing the ultimate effect—and thus will have no lines linking the two scenes together. When there are no lines linking one scene to the next and no sign of an earlier mention or foreshadowing, then objects, locations, and actions in and between scenes feel like they come out of the blue. Such a momentary lapse yanks readers out of the dream world you've so carefully created. Disoriented, they scan their story memories for the missing the link.

Notes:

_____

_____

_____

EMOTIONAL CAUSE AND EFFECT

Often writers create lots of zip and zing in the dramatic action but they zone out about the character's emotions. Other writers get carried away in passionately creating a binding historical and/or political timeline.

Mark on the Plot Planner those scenes when the character emotional plot is emotional, sensuous, and human.

Where is the linkage between the dramatic action and the character emotional development the weakest?

_____

_____

Summary

Clean up scenes. Expand scenes when needed. Cut when needed. Deepen every scene treatment of the characters, action, and theme.

The more often you stand back and analyze the sequence of scenes and how and where the energy rises and falls, the more your incomplete, hazy vision of a story will make sense. The action makes more sense. The protagonist is clearer to you. Each energetic marker shines.

As you did the first time around, work out the really big issues first. Tend to the details only when the plot and structure are set.

When you are certain that the core dramatic action plot, the character emotional development plot work, and the "vision" of your story is clear, go back and redo all the exercises again, this time keeping the finer, thematic details in mind at all times.

CHAPTER 14

FIND YOUR THEMATIC BUBBLE

Plot Whisperer Tweet: *When the dramatic action transforms the character over time, a story becomes thematically significant.*

A story exists through characters and the actions they take, but at the same time it also represents something else. To grasp what else your story represents and to be fully aware of its thematic significance before you have written a draft or two is usually premature. Far better is to wait until you understand the deeper meaning of your piece. When you do know what your story is about, every single decision you make in finessing a story from beginning to end becomes clearer, such as:

- Which plot line is primary and which are subplots
- What details to use to convey meaning
- The perfect crisis and climax and resolution

The Search for Meaning

To understand the world of a story in symbolic terms, use your imagination. Analyze each scene in your story for thematic elements, where the mood, metaphors, analogies, and descriptions show up and where you can insert or change symbols and meaning for the greatest good of the story.

As you analyze and plot and read and deliberate, challenge the underlying assumptions your story makes. Out of a vast array of possibilities, you choose to weave certain ideas and concepts into the fabric of your protagonist.

What would happen if you changed the imaginary lines in which you have boxed her?

_____

_____

_____

What rules does she break by entering the exotic world of the middle of the story?

_____

_____

_____

The portion of the story middle that builds to the crisis clarifies the most important themes of the book. As much as the themes in the middle deepen and contrast with earlier themes, they also foreshadow what comes at the climax at the end.

Often writers forget or miscalculate how long a story can take to write. The most effective way to keep your eye on the target without drowning in all the details is to keep the themes of your story uppermost in your mind.

Memoir Themes

My Stroke of Insight is the bestselling memoir by Jill Bolte Taylor, PhD. As a thirty-seven-year-old Harvard-trained neuroanatomist, Taylor writes what happens as she is hit with a massive stroke in the left hemisphere of her brain and about her journey to wellness.

In the introduction, the author stresses that the only reason she "endured the agony of recovery" was because of the responsibility she felt to help others. This statement begins the thematic significance of *My Stroke of Insight*.

In the beginning quarter of the story, set when she is well, Taylor explores the themes of responsibility, science, cognition, perception, trauma, loss, disintegration, death, adaptation, intuition, life, and peace. Each one of these themes helps to contrast the author's normal life from the exotic world of her stroke and foreshadows the challenges ahead.

Throughout the middle of *My Stroke of Insight*, nearly every theme presented in the beginning is deepened. We learn what responsibility, science, cognition, perception, trauma, loss, disintegration, death, adaptation, intuition, life, and peace mean now that she is no longer a Harvard doctor but has regressed to nearly an infant. Contrasted to her normal life, we understand the severity of the stroke and its challenges. To the themes in the beginning are now added: language, time, tranquility, judgment, helplessness, dependence, comprehension, communication, and surrender.

Jill recommits to her healing at the halfway point of the memoir when she goes home with her mother to prepare for surgery. With the introduction of the mother, an ally, the mood of the story shifts from despair to hope.

The portion of the middle that builds to the crisis brings into clarity the most important themes of the book. What started as themes of responsibility, science, cognition, perception, trauma, loss, disintegration, death, adaptation, intuition, life, and peace deepen through the context of change into language, tranquility, judgment, dependence, comprehension, communication, and surrender. When the stakes are at their highest as she prepares for surgery, themes narrow down to compassion, intuition, practice, and hope.

As much as the themes in the middle deepen and contrast with earlier themes, they also foreshadow what comes at the climax at the end.

The theme introduced in the introduction of Taylor's memoir echoes at the end, that of responsibility. The story stays true to that theme throughout the book. As much as the themes contrast and deepen and foreshadow what is coming at the end, they also point back to what came at the start.

Stories show a character changing, at the least, and transforming, at the most profound. This potential for growth reflects meaning. Meaning reflects truth. The thematic significance of a story shows what all the words in each individual scene add up to. At its best, the significance of a story connects each individual reader and audience member to a moment of clarity about our shared relationship to a bigger picture through a wider complex of thoughts and relationships that exist outside the story.

Thematic Significance Statement

The thematic significance of a story is a statement the story illustrates as truth. It can be plotted out scene by scene just as the dramatic action and the character emotional development are plotted out.

In Jodi Picoult's *New York Times* bestselling novel, *Change of Heart*, both Michael, the priest assigned to bring comfort to the death row inmate Shay Bourne, and Maggie Bloom, the district attorney assigned to uphold Shay's legal rights, are changed by the dramatic action in the story. Of the priest and the attorney, Maggie is actually transformed at depth by what happens and thus serves as the protagonist. Her emotional development brings thematic significance to the idea that a belief in the miraculous, full engagement in life, and acknowledgment of the truth leads to success in all things.

In the beginning of your work, plot scenes that introduce, define, and illustrate through dramatic action the individual elements of the story's thematic significance statement. These can include:

- Loss of family
- Rejection
- Abandonment
- Loyalty
- Responsibility
- Brothers and sisters, husbands and wives, mothers and daughters

The scene at the end of the beginning of the first quarter of *Change of Heart* shows Michael step across the threshold from his everyday life as a priest into a prison to comfort the man for whom, as a member of the jury, he voted the death penalty for.

Change Details to Reflect Thematic Significance

A story connects the everyday temporal world of sense perceptions to the realm of infinite knowledge. Physical details used in a scene can evoke a sensory awareness in the reader. The senses of sight, taste, hearing, touch, and smell connect with the reader and draw her more deeply into the story.

Sometimes an object in a story retains a protective power or special meaning and helps to reinforce the overall thematic significance of a story. This object(s), symbol, or metaphor can take the form of props or settings and enriching motifs.

Often in stories, the crisis that occurs around three-quarters of the way through the story happens in the protagonist's thematic hot spot, her cauldron, the place of ultimate transmutation.

Everything is a symbol of something in stories. Every metaphor, analogy, significant detail, and every single word serves more than one purpose.

Your Turn

In this chapter, you'll perform three exercises:

1. Create a thematic bubble chart.
2. Change up details on the Scene Tracker to reflect thematic significance.
3. Mark thematic significance points on your Plot Planner.

CREATE A THEMATIC BUBBLE CHART

The Thematic Bubble Chart illustrates the themes from our earlier example of *Change of Heart* by Jodi Picoult. Study how the themes in the smaller bubbles work together to form the Thematic Significance Statement in the center.

Next, fill in the themes of your story on the Thematic Bubble Chart, beginning with the smaller "bubbles" first.

Connect the circles to each other when relevant. Add new bubbles as new themes crop up. As you write, try to make a significant thematic statement as an action point. How *does* one do what the protagonist sets out to do in the story? Connect ideas together to create a broad thematic significance statement. Now, make the broad thematic significance statement relevant to your individual story. Tack on a phrase at the beginning or the end that qualifies, limits, or modifies the broader thematic significance as it applies to what happens in your story.

There are as many thematic significant statements as there are writers and stories.

When you come up with a thematic significance statement, even if it does not feel exactly right or ring 100-percent true, print the sentence in pencil in the large, center oval. With the statement in place, review the theme bubbles you created. Does the statement in the center oval include the major themes from the bubbles? If not, can you adapt the sentence to consist of more? Or adapt the themes in the bubbles so they more closely fit your overall theme?

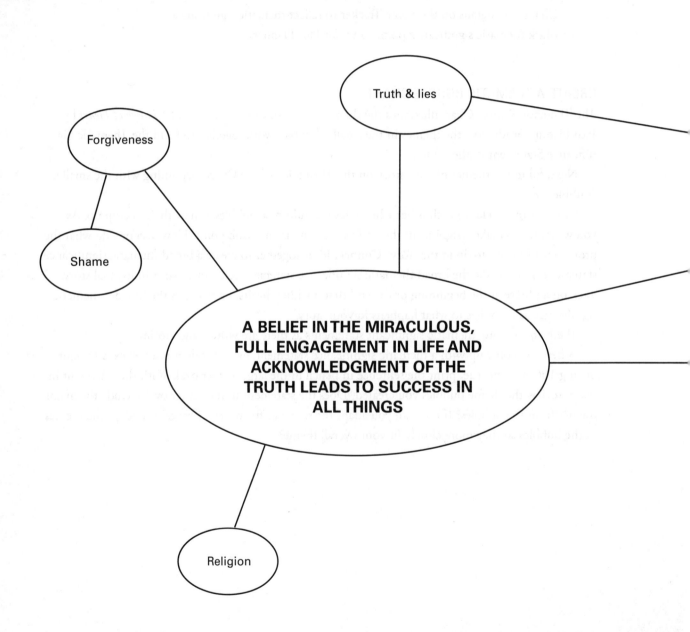

Figure 19. Thematic Significance Bubble Chart
Change of Heart by Jodi Picoult

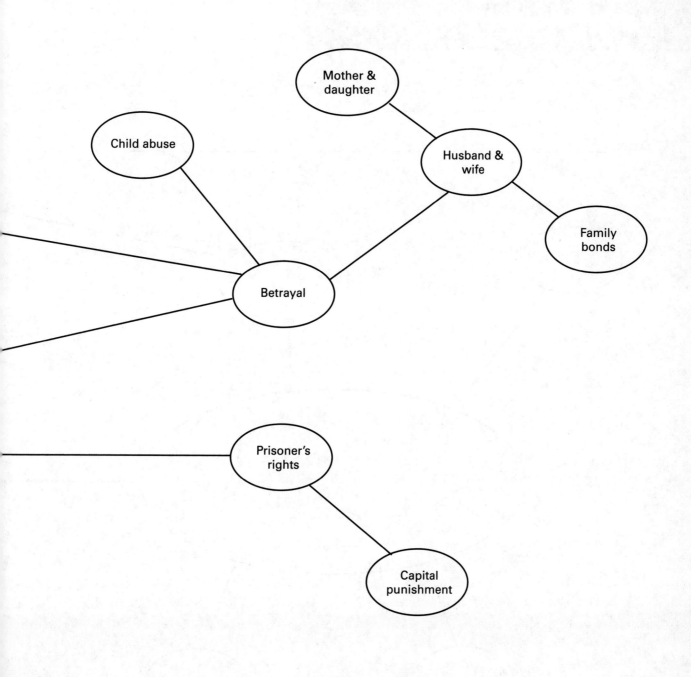

Figure 20. Thematic Significance Bubble Chart

Working Title: _____

Date: _____

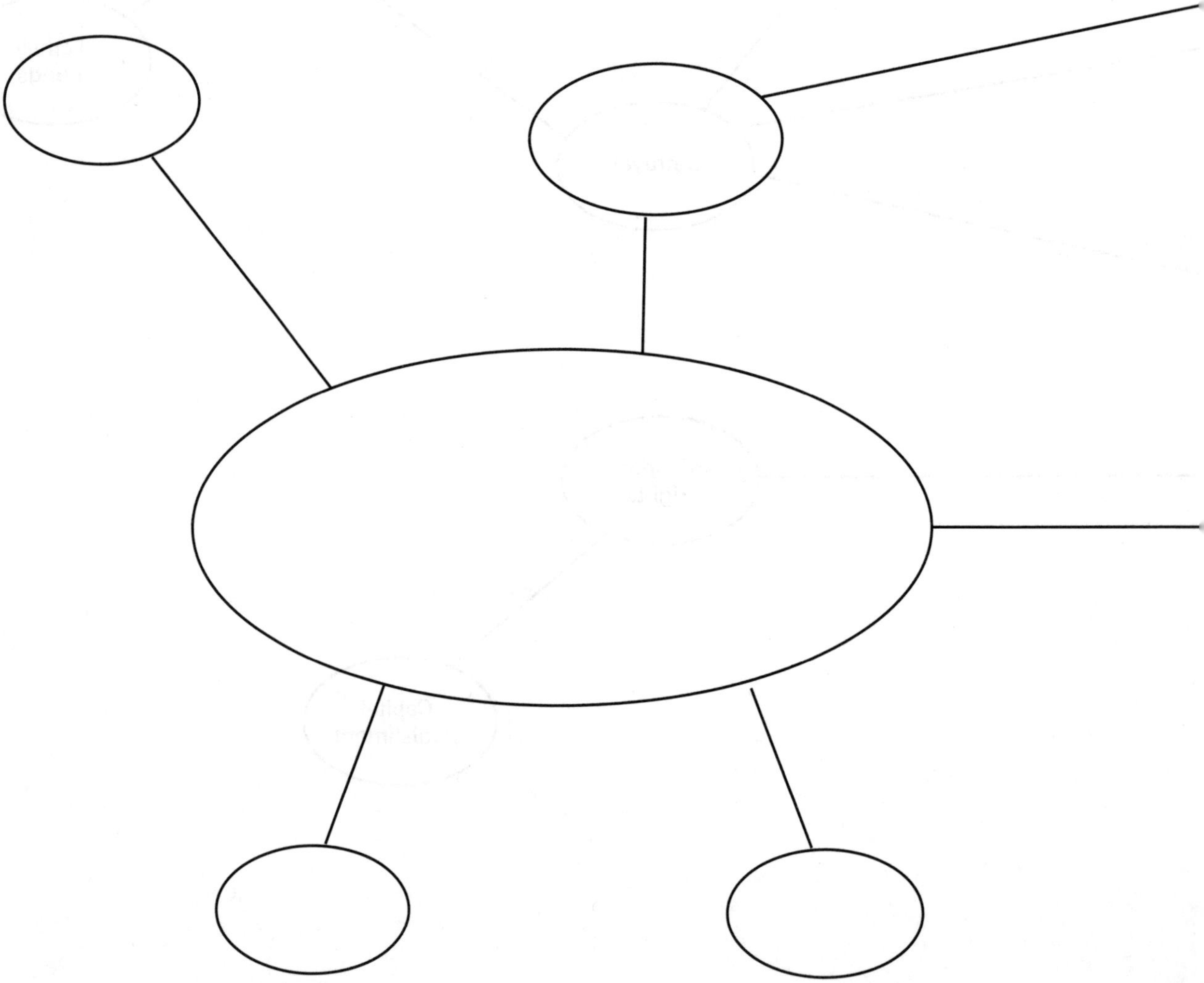

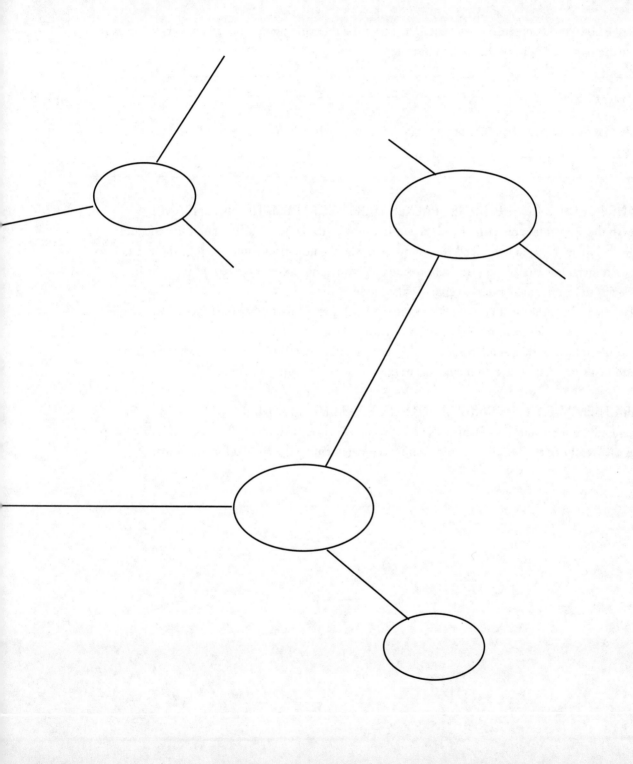

Describe how your book satisfies the requirements of the thematic significance statement. What does all the dramatic action in all the scenes illustrate?

_____

_____

What does the character's transformation symbolize about what she went through in the story?

_____

_____

CHANGE DETAILS ON THE SCENE TRACKER TO REFLECT THEMATIC SIGNIFICANCE

Refer to the last column on each of your Scene Trackers for the concrete details and thematic ideas you jotted there. Now, in light of all you know about the themes of your story, change those details so that each metaphor, each description reflects the thematic significance of the overall story. Switch up the details to just the right words to enhance the mood of the scene.

For example: A shoe in an early draft becomes a black leather assault boot in a story with themes of war, power, and domination. A shoe in an early draft becomes a flip-flop in a story with themes of comfort, impracticality, and nonconformity. A shoe in an early draft becomes a red Manolo Blahnik stiletto in a story that deals with themes of sex, power, and dominance.

MARK THEMATIC SIGNIFICANCE POINTS ON YOUR PLOT PLANNER

Make a notation on your Plot Planner wherever you find scenes with objects or metaphors or descriptions that reinforce the overall thematic significance statement you've created for your story.

CHAPTER 15

FINDING THE STRONGEST CLIMAX

Plot Whisperer Tweet: *It's going to take all your strength & your protagonist's, too, to lift your novel, memoir, screenplay to a climax.*

In the buildup to the climax of a story, the protagonist must keep her wits and strength about her. She may enter the final quarter of the story relatively weak. When she meets with an antagonist who is stronger than she is, the protagonist still can be knocked off course. When that happens, she is forced to readjust her course and follow an altered direction toward her goal. Still, during the entire final quarter of the story, the energy of the Universal Story moves steadily higher. Even when she meets up with a stronger force and needs a change of tactic, she is steadily climbing upward toward her goal.

The stronger the pressure is against her, the greater the strength the protagonist gains when she confronts and overcomes that force. The greater the force is against her, the bigger the change in her direction. The more dramatic the change in direction, the greater excitement and anticipation in the reader and audience.

The amount of power and strength, confidence and esteem gained and lost by the protagonist at the end and the degree of change in direction toward her goal determines when the energy of the story is at its greatest. As she gains more and more strength, her interactions will weaken her antagonists and may result in the actual destruction of her foes (internal and external). Finally, the words she speaks and the ideas she voices are heard and, for the first time, actually make an impact. The stronger the foe being destroyed by the protagonist makes for a stronger climax at the end.

A story is all about relationships. How a protagonist interacts with others in the beginning and the middle of the story predicts the self-knowledge she needs to gain to prevail at the end. Her relationship with nature, friends, family, community, her faith—or lack thereof—predicts the self-knowledge she needs for transformation. How she interacts with herself is the greatest predictor of all.

The protagonist suffers in the middle of the story to gain strength and courage and to learn to trust herself. To withstand modification and alterations, the protagonist must assess her values and the ideas she has been taught and her beliefs around those ideas. She must ultimately assess life itself and her part in it.

What Doesn't Work

I am often asked the number one problem writers have with plot. My answer varies, depending on the most recent plot consultation or plot workshop I've just done.

In general, though, the main plot problems writers struggle with are the climax and resolution.

So much time and thought and writing goes into developing a compelling protagonist with a mysterious backstory, deciding where is the exact right beginning of the story, how to make the action exciting and the book concept big, the details just right, the dialogue snappy, the setting exotic, the crisis disastrous.

I rarely (and I mean *rarely*) find a writer who has thoroughly thought out the climax and written the end quarter of the story as many times or more than the beginning.

Sure, writers bog down in the middle and thus the climax seems incredibly far away—nearly out of reach. By the time a writer limps her way to the climax, the story is lucky to have an ending at all, much less an ending that is meaningful and different and leaves the reader satisfied and wanting more.

The end of a romance novel, especially if it is for a teen, is so much more than "they lived happily ever after." You have been so careful not to use clichéd phrases, metaphors, and settings and have worked to make every element uniquely your own. Why settle for a trite ending?

When a character rises in triumph at the climax, what does she look like, act like? In the resolution, what does the world look like now that she is new and different and transformed and has shared the gift she came to share?

Everyone is looking for answers. Stories offer a new vision to replace the old, especially now that so much of the old world order falls apart.

Emotional Response

That fabulous beginning of your story and that wild twist in the middle do not count nearly as much to a reader as the end of the story. Sure, you hope she looks back and sees how everything is seamlessly tied together. In fact, what she's going to think about first is how the story ends.

Readers and audiences are affected first and foremost emotionally by the story they read, whether the story evokes fear or anger, joy and celebration, or sadness and resignation. Connecting with readers emotionally to the point they become instinctively involved in the story is the dream of every writer. The best place to search for this emotional effect is at the climax.

Think Different

Look beyond the words and sentences and scenes to the deeper pattern of your story. Every protagonist begins a story wanting something. The real reason that she goes after what she wants never (or rarely) is her stated reason. In fact, at the end of the story the protagonist can, and often does, fail at her stated goal. The reader cares because she knows the protagonist has actually won what she wanted and all that really matters is herself. She has gained self-knowledge and because of that she has been changed and transformed.

After having all of her layers stripped away one by one as false or unreliable, the protagonist reaches the point where she either must break down and live an unlived life or stand straight and rely on herself. To do that, first she must find the self on which she can rely. This is why often in a story, the protagonist's stated goal fades and is replaced by the *real* goal.

When the Climax Fails, the Reader Suffers

I analyzed one of my favorite books from my childhood, *The Secret Garden* by Frances Hodgson Burnett.

Plotting the scenes on a Plot Planner, I can see all the foreshadowing that shows up in the beginning of the story. In two short scenes, Mary, the ten-year-old protagonist, plays in dirt, attempting to plant cut flowers, each attempt foreshadowing the passion she will develop for the secret garden. Burnett also foreshadows the presence of another child in the house with the sound of crying three times before Mary actually discovers the cause of the cries.

In the middle of *The Secret Garden,* relationships abound. Mary's backstory reveals a childhood devoid of a true and loving relationship with others. In order to become who she is meant to be, she must heal this divide. Each relationship in the middle of the story becomes a subplot interconnected to all the other relationship plots.

Whenever the story seems to slow down or Mary's circumstances become too ideal, the author adds a plot twist to make for an exciting read. At the end of the story, the energy rises to a climax and thus, stays true to the needs of the Universal Story.

However—and this is an enormous however—rereading the book, having committed to Mary's story, I found an aspect of it unsatisfying. As soon as Mary, the transformed protagonist, helps Colin—the only son of the lord of the manor—heal and become whole, she moves into the shadows never to be heard from again. The last quarter of the book is all about Colin.

This is not so surprising when one considers that the book was published in 1911 (women didn't get the right to vote until 1920). In the political milieu of the days when the book was written, girls didn't have many options. Still . . . there is absolutely no climax or resolution for Mary's plot line and thus, no resolution for all the young girls who love(d) this book.

Perhaps years ago, women's options were confined to being a nurse, teacher, secretary, or mother. Now, a young girl's options are limitless. She can be a leader, an artist, a visionary, or an entrepreneur.

Writers today must reach, think differently, and stretch when it comes to writing the climax of a story. A protagonist's actions at the climax inspire the reader to think big and different and grow and evolve. Get the ending just right and deliver the greatest impact.

The Climax Setting

In *Faithful Place*, author Tana French suggests that Number 16 at the top of Faithful Place, an old abandoned house and the setting of two murders, holds the most energetic charge in the story. French uses Number 16 as the setting for the crisis and thus chooses to use a different story setting at the climax when Detective Frank confronts his greatest fear and the truth about his past.

For the climax scene, French uses an entirely new setting in the book, one the reader sees for the first time at the moment of greatest intensity in the entire story. Because the place where the climax plays out and the moment the entire story has been building to has never in the beginning or the middle or even in the buildup at the end been foreshadowed or mentioned, the climax plays out at a distance.

Not only is the reader not familiar with the setting, but the level of violence this calm-spoken detective demonstrates at the climax feels out of character. Sure, Frank is entitled to the release of pent-up emotions. Still, his actions confuse the reader and muddle the final outcome. The reader is left to ponder whether he is transformed by the dramatic action in the story and has exorcised his demons or if instead has awakened the sleeping giant?

Discarded along the Way

Often writers discard scene ideas for the climax, thinking they're not good enough, important enough, or worthy enough. After the work you've completed in this workbook, you may now see these discarded scenes in a different light. Perhaps you spot something of tremendous value in that scene you earlier abandoned. Now is a great time to explore those ideas that seemed once to hold no promise.

Stretch the boundaries of your current writing skills and risk trying something new for your climax. A fixed mindset about how a story should end is much less successful than a growth mindset. Some writers are afraid of what others will say about them if they write a climax that does not fit the image they portray to the outside world.

Push your abilities. Open up to new ideas. Take risks.

Expect some real climax failures as you come up with new ideas. Failures are a sign you have taken on a challenge. Taking on writing challenges expands your writing skills.

Your Turn

CLIMAX RE-EVALUATION CHECKLIST

Write a summary of the climax as you have envisioned the scene of greatest intensity in the entire story.

Indicate what happens in the climax with the following plot lines:

Dramatic action

_____

_____

_____

Character emotional development

_____

_____

_____

Thematic significance

_____

_____

_____

Any other major plot lines of the protagonist unanswered until the climax

_____

_____

_____

What themes does the climax deal with?

_____

_____

Where else are those same themes echoed in the story?

_____

_____

Make a list of all the endings you've written or simply imagined. Begin with the previous one. Add others. Include scenes you are sure have no value.

Notes:

_____

_____

_____

_____

Now go through the list you just generated, turn each ending on its ear. See the ending from a different angle or perspective. Strive to give the reader something new and fresh and miraculous. Write that.

Notes:

_____

_____

_____

_____

With the thematic bubble chart and the answers to the prompts at the end of Chapter 12, rewrite your climax three to five times. Each time stretch further than the time before. Be wild. Be bold. See what comes. Think outside the box.

Now, pick the scene that feels thematically to be the strongest version.

CHAPTER 16

JUST WHO ARE YOUR CHARACTERS, ANYWAY?

Plot Whisperer Tweet: *A story is about a character transforming her weaknesses into strengths.*

In Chapter 5 we discussed the impact a character's backstory has on her front story. Often something in her backstory caused a wound—either physical, psychic, or both. Anything in her past that now directly interferes with a character achieving her dream or goal in the front story is called a backstory wound.

The backstory wound can be conscious or forgotten. Either way, over time, a buildup of pain and suffering forms a burden on the protagonist's heart. Stories show a character shedding her backstory toward the end of the story and reawakening a belief in the miraculous.

Each protagonist has a fabulously valuable asset just waiting to be mined that she and most others don't even notice until she shrugs off her backstory, at least long enough to seize the prize at the end.

The wound can happen at any age and at any point at which the protagonist is diminished. Something occurs to mask the sense of the miraculous in the protagonist with thoughts and beliefs that reflect a misrepresentation of who she truly is. This illusory identity then becomes like a ghost structure and the basis for all of her future interpretations about life. As long as she defines her sense of self from old damage and as being less than extraordinary, she lives an unfulfilled life. A backstory wound is a lesser or greater trail of damage across her heart and limits her capacity for love.

Because a backstory is usually filled with fear, loathing, and pain, it is often buried. Thus, the backstory reveal toward the end of the middle of the story is often painful and difficult for the character to discern and integrate. Often, before a sense of freedom and a tranquil heart prevails, first comes forgiveness.

For the protagonist to complete her transformation at the end of the story, first she must reshape her center in herself and find stability in her own inner ground.

FOUR WAYS TO REVEAL A CHARACTER'S BACKSTORY WOUND
1. The story begins at the moment of loss and moves forward from there.
2. The story begins at the moment of loss and jumps in time where the front story begins.
3. The front story begins the story and the backstory is shown in flashback.
4. The front story begins the story and the backstory is shown through the character's behavior and the choices she makes.

Less than Perfect

The backstory wound makes the character less than perfect, which makes her believable and easier for readers and audiences to identify with. When a reader connects with what happens to the protagonist, she becomes united with that character in an intimate way. The audience's concern and compassion comes alive as they live the story.

One way for the reader to connect with the protagonist of your story is through her backstory wound.

DEVELOPMENT OF THE BACKSTORY WOUND
Untended and left to fester, the wound spins the protagonist into an unproductive repetition of behaviors and habits and patterns that doom her to failure. These unproductive habits are shown in various degrees in the beginning of the story.

In the middle of the story, as she is subjected to greater and greater complications, her backstory wound interferes in greater and greater measure.

After the crisis toward the end of the middle, she acknowledges the true source of her limitations—herself. Throughout the final quarter of the story, she struggles to trust, rely on, and be true to herself and find she has all she needs. Slowly she modifies her behavior, acting in a manner most natural to her. When she begins to use her innate abilities, life begins to improve for her. Freed from her self-imposed limitations, she seizes the prize at the end of the story.

Throughout the beginning, and especially the middle, the protagonist demonstrates what she is not able to do because of her beliefs. After the crisis, she exorcises the demons holding her back and synthesizes her old beliefs and experiences into what works for her.

In the final quarter of the story, she learns to use these newfound natural abilities more effectively. Each time she moves another step toward the climax, even if pushed back, she grows stronger and wiser. When she fails, she knows no more fear. She goes after her goal more intensely at the next opportunity. She comes to understand, learn about, and use her own talents, and can even adapt them to take advantage of the opportunities presented to her.

She finds that rather than manipulating others to get what she wants, she can find fulfillment by being herself and doing what is most natural for her.

Toward Transformation

The external action is a result of the protagonist's efforts moving forward toward her goal only to be blocked by the antagonists. This can be seen as an insistence that the protagonist find out the truth of her life, the mystery, the romance, the dilemma, the villain, or the murderer for herself. She no longer accepts someone else's word or a reality that is refracted through the lens of her backstory wound.

The ultimate test of cause and effect is to track the healing of the backstory wound as the character transforms through the course of the story. The healing of the backstory wound is unspoken but manifests itself through the transformed action taken by the protagonist. Whatever other gifts she seizes at the climax, an unspoken one is her newfound belief that her very presence in the world is itself the primal gift.

A Burden

Think of the protagonist's backstory wound as a burden she carries. That burden affects her passions and choices in jobs, in men, lifestyles, and all her habits.

The protagonists in the book examples we used in Chapters 1, 2, and 3 each have a backstory that reflects an unresolved tear or wound or confusion. Until this limitation is dissolved, the character cannot be who she is capable of being, who she longs to be, who she is meant to be—fully empowered with intuition, imagination, and creativity. Let's look briefly at these examples.

THE HELP

Both Aibileen and Skeeter are locked in the repetitive patterns of the past, acting in expected ways. Rather than heed the call for more, for different, for better choices, each of them is held back by fear. To have a life of her own choosing, Aibileen and Skeeter each have to face that fear.

Aibileen

A college-educated son gives Aibileen a belief in the miraculous. When he dies in a construction accident, she replaces her dreams of the future with the belief that white men at the site could have responded faster and saved her son. By the end of the story, Aibileen breaks free of the repetitive patterns of blaming and serving others and allows herself more in life.

Skeeter

The disappearance of her childhood maid causes Skeeter to falter. Constantine loved and believed in her while Skeeter's mother attended political meetings masked as social clubs. Until Skeeter solves the mystery of why Constantine left without saying goodbye and regains a sense of the miraculous, she remains stuck in repetitive patterns of the past.

MAJOR PETTIGREW'S LAST STAND

The major lost his sense of the miraculous when his father broke with tradition. When the major was just a young man, his father, rather than pass the two-gun hunting set to him, gave one of the guns to his younger brother. As a result of this psychic wound, the major remains trapped in the behaviors created in his youth.

ESPERANZA RISING

Esperanza's sense of self is stripped when she and her mother are forced to leave their past for an uncertain future. As long as Esperanza identifies with her lost possessions and position in life, she struggles.

A character's backstory wound, once exposed soon after the crisis, can inform the protagonist of her emotional attachment to the past. Facing the full truth, she is no longer dislocated from herself. She begins to truly feel. Her burden diminishes and a new lightness enters her body, enough to propel her into the end of the story.

Backstory Wounds of the Heart

Some wounds are deep; emotional more than physical. In reviewing the wounds suffered by your protagonist, keep the following in mind:

- A timid heart gives little.
- A fearful heart holds back.
- A heavy heart is dark and regretful.
- A judgmental heart judges not only others but herself and never comes out well.
- An unforgiving heart blames.
- An angry heart resists.
- A guilty heart hides.
- An addictive heart cares only about herself.
- A hateful heart kills the spirit of possibilities in relationships with others.

RECOGNIZE PATTERNS

Whatever causes the protagonist's backstory wound determines the mood and theme of the story. If the wound is deep and caused by violence and trauma, the story will be deep, violent, and traumatic. If the wound is more superficial and caused by confusion or miscommunication, the story will have elements of confusion and deal with themes of communication.

Each decision and choice the protagonist makes throughout the story is based on the beliefs she developed based on her backstory wound. Train yourself not only to recognize patterns when they show up, but to intensify them incrementally.

At its deepest level, a story is about a protagonist reuniting with her true, courageous, light and free, compassionate, and loving heart.

Your Turn

BACKSTORY CHECKLIST

Write a short account (no more than 150 words) of the backstory wound.

_____

_____

_____

_____

How does that wound show itself in your protagonist's decision-making process?

_____

_____

List the habits and repetitive patterns she has created for herself to compensate for her backstory wound:

_____

_____

_____

_____

How do these patterns interfere with her gains toward what she most wants in life?

_____

_____

CHAPTER 17

THE END OF THE BEGINNING AND THE BEGINNING OF THE END

Plot Whisperer Tweet: *Beginnings hook readers. Endings create fans.*

Beginnings predict how the story will end. The end of your story reflects that determination. Always ask yourself if there is something you can change at the beginning and/or at the end to bring more contrast and an unexpected result. Strive for that something different that makes your readers think.

In some stories, the protagonist takes a significant risk in return for a small chance at earning a big reward. In other stories, the protagonist is interested in a lesser reward for less of a risk. Beyond standard responses is the story that challenges traditional assumptions to create as much value as possible.

Here, close to the end of the workbook, see your story with fresh eyes and identify opportunities to generate new ideas, new beginnings that reflect new endings and new ways of looking at the world. Compare the beginning and the end, searching for the creative solutions sitting right in front of you in the scenes. This will mean stepping back and looking at your story more broadly. Take off the blinders and see an entire world of possibilities by comparing what happens at the beginning of your story to what happens at the end.

Consider your beginning and ending now as examples of a fine beginning and ending. At the same time, acknowledge that what you've envisioned is only one of an almost infinite number of beginnings and endings you can write for a story. The first few beginnings and endings you imagine and write may end up sounding clichéd, traditional, and expected. Don't restrict yourself to visualizing your story sounding like all the ones you've read and watched at the movies. Instead, consider a world of possibilities.

We are all heavily influenced by the stories we read and hear and by the people around us, especially those who like to tell others what to do with a story. We all receive explicit and implicit messages about the roles our characters are expected to play, and too often we fall prey to traditional endings. We are powerfully influenced by the messages around us and embedded into our environment.

Each time you step back and compare the beginning and the end with an eye for creative solutions, you spot another idea.

Separate yourself from the beginning and ending you want for the story and explore what beginning and ending the story wants for itself. You have been asked in this workbook to make decisions about your story and then stick with them through the relentless pursuit of plotting your story from beginning to end.

Now is the time to reconsider your choices, always being on the lookout for beginnings and endings that do not fit the expected results and lead to uncharted territory. Latch on to anomalies. These are where true breakthroughs are made. Keep searching for other viable alternatives to your story choices. Take a risk by stepping off the clearly defined path and exploring a new beginning or a new ending or both.

Most events snap into focus when you look at them in retrospect. When you are plotting and writing, the way forward is always fuzzy and full of uncertainty. Now as you look back on all the scenes at the beginning, middle, and end, the story makes perfect sense.

Though your protagonist starts out the story with a goal, the rest of the story exposes her to a wide array of opportunities.

Ramp up your observational skills. Tap into your talents and those of your protagonist. Unlock creativity to identify problems you may have spotted in your story early on but never thought to solve. Unearthing common problems that are not usually thought of and then working out a way to solve it in a story brings fans.

Now that you have plotted your story from beginning to end and analyzed the beginning, middle, and end, pull back even further to view the beginning in relationship to the end and the end in relationship to the beginning.

A Path of Wonder

Each story begins on a path of wonder where something significant in the life of the protagonist gradually unfolds and becomes visible both to herself and to the reader.

You begin a story with a character in possession of a flaw, a fault, a hang-up, or a prejudice. You give her the rest of a story to get over her weaknesses. A comparison of the character from the beginning with the one at the end shows whether she fails to overcome her flaw or succeeds at getting over her hang-up.

Raymond Carver begins his story, "Cathedral," with a nasty, prejudiced, narrow-minded man who hates anyone and everyone different. By the end of the story, this same man, having discovered we are more alike than different, becomes emotionally connected to and feels a bond of community together with a man he once would have scorned.

THE BEGINNING OF THE BEGINNING

First line, first paragraph, first chapter . . . each one draws the reader from one sentence to the next.

The beginning awakens the protagonist and challenges her to change. The beginning holds clues to everything that follows in the story. On the other hand, the ending often sneaks up on the protagonist. She is so into the moment-to-moment action of the story that when she arrives at the end of her journey she is startled to see anew. Often, before she disappears into the folds of time, the story brings her back to that which was nearest all along, as is the case with the young protagonist in *The Alchemist* by Paulo Coelho. At the end of the story, Santiago finds a chest of jewels and gold buried under the same tree back home where he had his original dream that triggered the adventure in the beginning.

When the protagonist returns, she has changed and is no longer the one that left in the first place. Often, because the protagonist is now healed and has broken out of the mundane and everyday rituals of life, she can no longer live in the constricted mode of the cramped and shabby past.

Whether stumbling or rumbling, marching or tiptoeing, the protagonist moves toward her destiny. At the same time, the end silently travels nearer and nearer until it arrives. The end shows the protagonist as more than she was at the beginning.

SETTING AT THE BEGINNING AND THE END

The setting of a story is either positive or negative. In a positive setting, good things happen to the protagonist or the environment is good, wholesome, or beautiful. In contrast, in a negative setting bad things happen to the protagonist or it is frightening or ugly. Darkness and bleak landscapes as in the opening pages of Edgar Allan Poe's "The Fall of House of Usher" create the mood and tone that sets the story in motion. Setting can be revelatory of virtually any element in the story and reinforces the overall theme of the story.

Your Turn

Fill in the plot point comparison chart for the beginning and the end of your story based on your Plot Planners.

SETTING

Describe in a couple of sentences the setting at the beginning of your story.

_____

_____

_____

_____

Describe in a couple of sentences the setting at the end of your story.

_____

_____

_____

_____

Compare the two settings. How do they complement, foreshadow, contrast, and reflect each other?

_____

_____

_____

What do the two settings represent to and about the protagonist?

_____

_____

_____

_____

Reconsider where and when to begin your story (this will affect the divisions and where the energetic markers arrive). If necessary, revise the scene placement.

_____

_____

_____

_____

THEMES

List the themes at the beginning quarter of your story.

_____

_____

_____

_____

List the themes at the final quarter of your story.

_____

_____

_____

_____

Do any of the symbols, metaphors, or similes used to convey the themes just listed appear in both the beginning and the end?

_____

_____

_____

_____

PROTAGONIST

Name:

_____

Which trait(s) of the character directly impacts the climax of the story?

_____

_____

How was that trait introduced at the beginning?

_____

What skills and knowledge and abilities does she need for success at the climax?

_____

_____

Which of these are missing at the beginning?

_____

_____

SECONDARY CHARACTERS

List the major secondary characters in the beginning by name:

_____

_____

_____

_____

List the major secondary characters by name in the end:

_____

_____

_____

_____

Circle any secondary characters who appear both in the beginning and the end.

What aspects of the protagonist do the secondary characters reflect at the beginning of your story?

_____

What attributes and/or traits, behaviors and/or beliefs do the secondary characters have that reflect what the protagonist needs to learn to prevail at that climax?

_____

How does what the secondary characters represent at the beginning of the story contrast to what they represent at the end?

_____

_____

What aspects of the protagonist that are foreshadowed at the beginning are in stark contrast with what the secondary characters reflect at the end of your story?

_____

_____

CONCLUSION

As I considered how to conclude this book, a great gnarly spider dropped from the ceiling into the ficus I have draped over my computer for balance. The spider, black and huge when crawling across the white ceiling, immediately blended and disappeared into the greenery.

I was just reading about spiders as I pondered relationships for Chapter 15. Ted Andrews says in *Animal Speak* that a spider's geometric form is of the figure eight and infinity:

"Spider teaches you to maintain a balance—between past and future, physical and spiritual, male and female. Spider teaches you that everything you now do is weaving what you will encounter in the future . . . has to do with rhythms—the rise and fall, the flow and flux."

This feature is like the rise and fall and the flow and flux and rhythm of the Universal Story.

Writing does not mean putting aside your head to write from the heart. Instead, writing is an expression of the emotional and the logical coming together.

As I write these words, the spider reveals itself again. This time, it is actually on my desk and headed straight at me. "Everything you do now is weaving what you will encounter in the future."

My hope is that the exercises in this workbook stimulate your imagination and fire your passion to write.

Feedback from writers about *The Plot Whisperer: Secrets of Story Structure Any Writer Can Master* inspires me to acknowledge and thank the courage of *women writers everywhere resurrecting their dreams*. Women have told me that *The Plot Whisperer* has also acted as a catalyst to those who have stopped writing but never forgot the dream.

While I was writing this workbook, books from my childhood that influenced my thinking kept popping up for examination. So many of them represent a patriarchal point of view about women and our roles and expectations in society.

I am passionate about women's voices coming to the fore. Our left-brained, logical, and linear world of today deserves the balance that can only come when paired equally with a right-brained, holistic, and intuitive approach. Women hold that key.

Yikes! I've got to do something about that spider. She looks huge and determined.

I return with a clear glass and card. No sign of the spider. I invite her forward so I can save her and her babies can be born in the wilds of my urban neighborhood. I peek under the clutter of books and papers on my desk. I liked it better when I could see her.

This workbook may prove to be most challenging to the very writers I hope to inspire. Many women writers find plot and structure counterintuitive . . . until seen through the Universal Story.

If it were simple to write the perfect novel, memoir, or screenplay there would be a lot more people doing just that. The truth is, writing can be difficult. It involves craft and passion and more than a bit of magic.

My dream is that by facing the challenges in the book, you will dig deep. Think different. Surrender to the journey. You have everything you need to succeed. Enjoy the ride.

ACKNOWLEDGMENTS

Special thanks to Peter Archer for suggesting the idea of this workbook and then so effortlessly, or so it felt like, making it happen. Thank you to everyone at Adams Media.

Thank you to Jill Corcoran for your generous support.

Thanks also to all the writers who have offered comments and feedback after using the Scene Tracker, Plot Planner, and Thematic Bubbles and all the other exercises in this workbook. I want to especially acknowledge and thank the courage of women writers everywhere resurrecting their dreams.

Finally, thank you to the man of my dreams and my everyday life, my husband, Bobby Ray Alderson.

ABOUT THE AUTHOR

Drawing from two decades of experience as a speech, language, and learning disability therapist for children, Martha Alderson started teaching plot workshops in 1997. Also known as the Plot Whisperer, Martha Alderson is the author of *The Plot Whisperer: Secrets of Story Structure Any Writer Can Master*. She also wrote *Blockbuster Plots Pure & Simple* (Illusion Press) and several e-books on plot as well as creating the Scene Tracker Kit. As an international plot consultant for writers, Martha's clients include bestselling authors, New York editors, and Hollywood movie directors. She teaches plot workshops to novelists, memoirists, and screenwriters privately, at plot retreats, through writing clubs and chapter meetings, and at writers' conferences where she takes writers beyond the words and into the very heart of a story.

As the founder of Blockbuster Plots for Writers: *www.blockbusterplots.com* and December, International Plot Writing Month: *www.plotwrimo.com*, Martha manages the award-winning blog for writers: *www.plotwhisperer.com*, honored by Writers Digest in 2009, 2010, 2011, and 2012. Her vlog, How Do I Plot a Novel, Memoir, Screenplay?, covers twenty-seven steps to plotting your story from beginning to end: *www.youtube.com/user/marthaalderson*.

She lives in Santa Cruz, California, and frequently travels around the country to teach plot workshops.